365 Glorious Nights of Love and Romance

365 Glorious Nights of Love and Romance

Patrika Darbo
with Lorraine Zenka

ReganBooks
An Imprint of HarperCollinsPublishers

HarperCollins books may be purchased for educational, business, or sales promotional use. For information please write: Special Markets Department, HarperCollins Publishers Inc., 10 East 53rd Street, New York, NY 10022.

FIRST EDITION

Designed by Kris Tobiassen

Printed on acid-free paper

Library of Congress Cataloging-in-Publication Data

Darbo, Patrika.
    365 glorious nights of love and romance / Patrika Darbo with Lorraine Zenka.—1st ed.
        p.   cm.
    ISBN 0-06-001382-6 (hc)
        1. Sex instruction for women. 2. Sexual attraction. 3. Self-confidence.
    4. Body image in women. 5. Darbo, Patrika. 6. Overweight women—
    United States—Biography. 7. Actresses—United States—Biography.
    I. Title: Three hundred sixty-five glorious nights of love and romance.
    II. Zenka, Lorraine.   III. Title.

HQ46 .D35 2002
306.4—dc21   2002017333

02   03   04   05   06   ❖/RRD   10   9   8   7   6   5   4   3   2   1

To my husband, Rolf—
My friend, my partner, my life.
I love you.

Contents

Preface

There's no point in thinking, "Coulda, woulda, shoulda." I'm where I'm supposed to be, with no regrets. I've learned that power is sexy. So is confidence in yourself. Whatever package you're in, put a bow on it. Get out there and capture your dreams!

Playing a popular sexpot vixen, Nancy Wesley, on NBC TV's *Days of Our Lives* has been a wonderful and eye-opening experience for me. I dove into a sea of size-two soap opera starlets and created a tidal wave of heartwarming response from the press and public that stunned me.

So I'm very happy that social-climbing, plus-size Nancy—together with *Days'* writers' intelligent story lines—gave me the material to earn a Daytime Emmy Award nomination in 2001. I've landed other kudos, too: *Soap Opera Digest*'s Outstanding Female Newcomer, 1999, and the wonderfully irreverent title of "Full-Figured Bitch Goddess of Daytime" when *TV Guide* and *Entertainment Tonight* jointly named me among TV's "Sixteen Sexiest Stars."

I'm thrilled that I can play one of the most dynamic characters on television—day or night. On-screen, Nancy is loved, adored, and treated like a queen by her handsome, hunky husband who has svelte Barbie types swooning at his feet. But Dr. Wesley has eyes only for sexy, sassy, full-bodied Nancy. Go, Craig!

I want you to listen to me when I tell you that sexy self-confidence comes in all shapes and sizes. I'm going to put myself out on a limb here, in this book, and share some of my most personal experiences and hard-won victories. You'll learn some things about me you didn't know before. Hopefully, you'll learn a lot about yourself through these pages, too. I'll throw out some down-home advice, not so much for losing weight but for gaining confidence, developing a winning attitude, and maintaining a positive—even sexy—approach to life. I'm not telling anyone to change, but to simply celebrate who you really are. If I can, you can.

Thankfully, I'm respected for my work in many areas of TV and film. I have a great husband, a solid marriage, and a good life. I like where I am and how I've gotten here, personally and professionally. My life's not perfect. I've made mistakes, but I've made many right moves, too. I know who I am. I took hold of my dreams and made them reality. Others can, too.

Like many other people's childhoods and adolescences, mine held its share of relocation, isolation, and intimate pain. Then, as an adult, I chose one of the toughest, rejection-filled professions on earth: acting. At every turn, I chose a combination of courage, openness, and belief in myself to build confidence as I made my dreams reality.

My biological dad, a nightclub manager, was called Chubby even though his given name was Harold. No one ever called him that; his name was Chubby. My stepdaddy, Donald Davidson, who my mom, Patricia, married when I was about ten, was the traveling secretary and publicist for the then Milwaukee Braves. He was a dwarf, and his humor and success as a businessman and human being inspired me.

We are all so different yet have so much in common in our hearts and souls. If we were all blind, would there be any differences? Would we know from the sound of the voices we hear that one person is fat, another is black, or is thin, or has a pockmarked face, or is missing an arm? Sometimes we need to close our eyes to see the real person.

I didn't start out power-savvy or self-confident and I still have a lot to learn. Along with many obesity experts, I found that childhood hurts and being a "people pleaser" led to an inappropriate relationship with food as I stuffed down my unexpressed emotions. Chocolate cake never makes you choose, and sometimes it seems to take away the pain. Food was there for me when my parents were not.

After my parents' divorce, my brother, Danny, went to live with our dad and his new wife. My sister, Peggy, and I lived with our paternal grandmother and saw our mom on her one day off from work as a restaurant host. Grandma's fried pork chops and fruit pies were delicious and comforting. So were my lonely-time snacks, which were all the sweeter for their secrecy. My candy-bar wrappers were shoved between the mattresses or littered my locker at school. I gained weight, and was put on diets by both my mother and grandmother by the time I was eight or nine. I felt that they were taking their love away again.

School was not a time of dating and nonstop good times. There were name-calling and nasty remarks, but I always tried to turn each situation into a good-natured joke. I became everybody's pal, everybody's friend, from the football player to the science or German club member. I got along very well in school. I decorated the gym. But I didn't go to the prom.

Over the years, I've been up and down the scale often, reaching 220 pounds and torturing myself to my lowest weight, 140. However, through diets and binges, I didn't allow myself to lose sight of my dreams. I developed a great survival instinct that helped me think on my feet, throw a quick, witty retort, and eventually led me, as an adult, to my acting career, an arena filled with challenge, rejection, and the eventual thrill of acceptance. Becoming an actor saved me. As a child, I became manipulative. I learned how to be what other people wanted me to be in order to survive, to get my way, to be liked.

I learned to master healthy manipulation and make-believe as I attended the Atlanta School of Drama, then moved to Los Angeles in the early 1970s. I worked as a credit manager while performing in community theater in Burbank. That's where I met Rolf Darbo, who was then a film-production manager for Disney. I knew after our first date that I would marry him.

Soon after meeting Rolf, my career hit the fast lane and I left my conventional day job behind in 1984. I had a lot of fun and proved that a large woman can be physically agile. There was a time when I was nearly naked and was suspended from a crane in a harness outside the fifth-floor window of a burning building, and another time when I was painted blue. I landed acting jobs one after another. Only one casting director ever suggested that I lose weight. Although I went up and down the scale at different times, being big, beautiful, and bold made others recognize that I had talent. I had to be myself, and it paid off. You'll learn that, too.

While I'm at it, let me tell you about my movie credits. I worked with John Malkovich in *In the Line of Fire*, Christine Lahti and Meg Tilly in *Leaving Normal*, Whoopi Goldberg in *Corrina, Corrina*, and was heard as the third sheep in *Babe*. I costarred, playing the character of Marlene Turnover with Beau Bridges and Judge Reinhold in the critically acclaimed film *Daddy's Dyin'* . . . *Who's Got the Will?* I originated that last role onstage in 1987 at Theater/Theater in Los Angeles. For my work in the film adaptation, I was awarded the Golden Cane best actress award at the

International Comedy Film Festival in Vevey, Switzerland. Some of my other films include *Midnight in the Garden of Good and Evil, It Takes Two, Space Invaders, Gremlins II, The Burbs, Troop Beverly Hills, The Night Before, Ghost Dad, Speed 2,* and *Durango Kids.*

In TV movies, I played a title role in the NBC movie of the week, *Roseanne and Tom: Behind the Scenes,* and costarred in *The Ruby Bridges Story* for Disney/ABC.

My episodic television work includes *Step By Step,* as a regular, plus guest spots on *L.A. Doctors, Seinfeld, Mama's Family, Growing Pains, Roseanne, Sisters, Grace Under Fire,* and *The George Carlin Show.* I did a lot of commercials, too. The longest-running one was for Tetley tea.

NOW, *DAYS'* NANCY IS THE DRIVING FORCE BEHIND HANDsome and charismatic Dr. Craig Wesley. As the duo, we skillfully lied, schemed, and manipulated to make Dr. Wesley chief of staff at Salem University Hospital. Nancy and Chloe (the child Nancy gave up at birth) were reunited, but their mother-daughter bond continues to be less than ideal. The role has rarely made an issue of weight. Nancy has broken the size barrier, and I'm happy she's shattered the stereotype of heavy people who are laughed at, beat up, or put down. I would never, never play a role that would make fun of someone fat.

I've learned never to let momentary fear stand in my way. There are no excuses: I'm short, round, and redheaded. That's about it. When I'm a little less round, I'm pleasingly plump. Yes, I have my own self-esteem problems. So what? I'm overweight. I'm pretty. I'm talented. And I'm sexy. I would not be where I am right at this moment if I were not. I've gotten here by not letting anyone else set my limits or tell me what my life should be.

Twenty years from now, we will be twenty years older, with or without the career or lifestyle we wanted, our dreams fulfilled or turned to dust. It's our choice. Listen to your true inner voice. It's the one that loves you, encourages you, and nurtures you. It gives you that little extra push, and protects you.

I'M INVITING YOU INTO MY PRIVATE WORLD NOW. I WANT to help you remember the best of who *you* are. It matters little if you want to be an actor or a marine biologist, find a better job or a loving husband or lover. Leave excuses like "First I have to lose five or fifty pounds," "Let my hair grow," "Be rich" behind. Take the courses you've talked about, join a club, learn to dance.

Have your goals, make a plan, and go for it. Enjoy life, your sensuality, and your spirit. Whatever your individual package, put a bow on it. Get out there and capture your dreams. If I can, you can!

—PATRIKA DARBO

PART I
About Nancy and Me

1

Let Me Introduce Myself

"What makes you so special?"

A male reporter once asked me this question. He wanted to know why, in this era of underfed, rail-thin actresses, I get roles that have nothing to do with my size. Stung by his candor, I was tempted to lash back, "What makes you so rude?" Instead, I smiled sweetly and answered, "Aside from my talent, I think I've gotten work because I get along with people, I report to the set on time, and I know my lines. I'm a complete professional. Basically, I enjoy what I do, and, from what people tell me, it shows." I resisted adding, "I'm thrilled to be me!"

So why am I so damn happy? you might wonder. I'm married to a wonderful man who ravages me with love and affection, I have a close circle of good, dependable friends, and I play what I consider to be the most exciting role in daytime television—the shrewd and sensuous Nancy Wesley on NBC TV's longest-running drama series, *Days of Our Lives.*

Now, before you start to resent my good fortune, remember that it took a lot of hard work to get where I am today. Of course, I want to enjoy it. And since you, dear friend, plunked down your hard-earned cash to read my story, I intend to share the secrets of my success, both professionally and personally.

Early in my acting career, I made a decision to not play roles that were targets of gratuitous fat people jokes. If I was asked to do something that I didn't think was funny, or was insulting to over-weight people, I'd respectfully pass on it. Many actors live by the creed "Work is work," and friends of mine would admonish, "Someone's going to play the part. Besides, it could lead to your lucky break and make you a star!" They couldn't understand that I didn't want stardom on those terms. That would fill me with self-loathing because I'd be cashing in on a cruel, cheap stereotype that belittled my overweight brothers and sisters.

Let me climb onto my soapbox. As a society, we're expected to be politically correct about race, religion, sexual orientation, physi-cal handicaps, social class—you name it. The line stops at over-weight people. Look what happens when a person hits the news who's bigger than the ideal size, especially if there's a whiff of scan-dal involved. Monica Lewinsky (who I'm told is a *Days of Our Lives* fan) is a prime example. Her size was mentioned far more often than that soiled blue dress she kept hidden in her closet. Her girth was fair game for the mean-spirited punch line. Elizabeth Taylor and Oprah find every rise and fall in their weight makes head-lines—and unflattering tabloid photos, too.

Even worse than lame stand-up comics, with their desperate one-liners, are the larger people I see being the first ones to make fun of themselves. I understand that it's a defense mechanism, the theory being that it would hurt more coming from someone else.

But in the long run, being first with the ridicule is far more destructive to our own self-esteem, and the image we project to others, than the nasty barbs expressed on a late-night TV talk show. So that is why—I'm getting off my soapbox now—I don't do fat jokes.

In 1992, I was a series regular on the television sitcom *Step By Step*, which starred Suzanne Somers and Patrick Duffy. I played Suzanne's sister, Penny. In one episode, I had a scene with Patrick and a creepy-crawly spider. I was supposed to be frightened by the spider and run around in circles. Instead, I suggested that it would be more likely that a woman frightened by the sight of a spider would probably jump into the protective arms of the nearest man. The director agreed to give it a try. Patrick, who played my brother-in-law, Frank, was also game. Now, this is a guy who was used to working with Suzanne Somers, queen of the ab cruncher. With me acting as her stand-in, it was as if the weights on his exercise equipment had suddenly doubled. When we performed the scene, I could feel the trembling strain in Patrick's arms. But he never let on that it was a struggle for him. Patrick would never hurt his TV sister-in-law's feelings, and I appreciated his noble behavior. In fact, to this day, every time I see his friendly face on my TV screen, I blow him a kiss.

Full disclosure: Yes, I've taken advantage of my size to get a part. In 1989, on another TV sitcom, *Growing Pains*, I played a mother hosting a Halloween party. The character really got into the spirit of trick or treat; her wardrobe was like Elvira's, so I was tightly trussed into my costume. You could have served dinner on my chest. A representative from ABC's standards and practices department—also known as the censors—took one look at me and advised, "Leash those puppies up." Of course, before any modifications were made on the costume, he wanted a photo of himself with me, and, as he so eloquently phrased it, "those puppies."

Directors and other actors are often surprised to find that I'm very agile and athletic. Over the course of five seasons, I played three different characters on *Growing Pains.* In a 1988 episode titled "Graduation Day," Mike, played by Kirk Cameron, was graduating from high school. I was the keeper of the diplomas. The director wanted to shoot the scene to make it look as if I had slipped, and as I was falling, the diplomas would be tossed into the air. His plan was to cut away so I wouldn't have to do anything more than start to fall, and then, when the camera was on me again, I'd already be on the floor. I told him that though I'm large, I was certain I could perform the actual fall without hurting myself. He let the cameras roll. I stumbled, threw the diplomas into the air, flew like Superman, and then glided across the floor as if I was on a Slip 'n Slide. I'm proud to say it was a scene of perfectly timed, exquisite beauty. Only, we had to shoot it again. Kirk was so stunned by what he had seen that he totally blanked on his lines. Fortunately, the second attempt was as perfect as the first. If you ever come across a rerun of the episode, watch closely and you'll notice that Kirk is fighting not to burst out laughing.

When I did a commercial for Sony's PlayStation, I was strapped in a harness and hoisted up by a crane to the outside of a fifth-floor window, the building in blazes. Although a stuntwoman took the fall from the fifth-floor window for most of the drop sequence, I stepped in and performed a controlled fall from the second story. Hey, I'm competitive and I love a challenge.

As an actress, I will do what's necessary and appropriate to secure work. In 1988, I had an audition for a commercial starring Pee-wee Herman. It was for his talking Pee-wee doll. The part was an island native so I went to the audition wearing a leopard top over a pair of sweatpants that I had cut above the knee in jagged edges. It looked as if I was wearing a loincloth. To top it off, I teased my hair and stuck a large dog bone in the top of it. I got the role immediately.

On the day of the shoot, I had to be up at the crack of dawn. While driving to the location, a beach near Malibu, the emerging sunlight invigorated my heavy eyelids. At the location, the other sleep-deprived actors and actresses and I were given grass skirts, coconut shells, and other various odd items to make us look like exotic (no, make that bizarre) island people like no others. To top off the ensemble, we were painted blue—a complete surprise to everyone. It wasn't your basic navy, aqua, or sky blue, either. Instead, we were transformed by an electrifying coat of neon blue paint. And we wore blond wigs. Talk about getting the sleep out of your eyes! The visual was absolutely wacky. Picture the Flintstones, stranded on Gilligan's Island and dropping acid. Pee-wee didn't want to insult any particular ethnic group in any way so he invented another.

I played the island tribal chieftain's daughter. So, I also got a headdress, in addition to the grass skirt, and a bra made from coconut shells, each of which, incidentally, was about the size of a dime. I thought to myself, "What is this supposed to be? Nipple decorations?" I knew that if I put on the would-be Wonderbra, we'd have an X-rated commercial on our hands. "Excuse me," I said to the director, "but one size does not fit all." So I asked for bigger coconuts. Even though I was requesting a major alteration on my costume, I bravely stood before him, blue from head to toe, my hair pinned under a skullcap. What did I have to lose? Wardrobe took my tiny pink coconuts and strategically added several rows of large, multicolored feathers around them. It did the trick but it looked as if the NBC peacock had collided with my coconuts.

The group of actors I was with, the "natives," came in all shapes and sizes. I noticed that some of the larger men had breasts nearly as big as mine. But of course they were not given coconuts, or feathers.

As a bunch, we were a broad spectrum of diverse personalities, as you'd probably find with any random group. Early in the day, we milled about in small clusters, either in the parking lot or by the dressing areas, chatting with the crew, the caterers, anyone who was around. However, as soon as each of us was painted blue, one by one we began to cluster together. We felt too "different" among the non-painted people and, I'd bet, we were subconsciously protecting ourselves from ridicule in much the same way some overweight people isolate themselves. Even at lunch, all the blue people huddled at one table. There was comfort in belonging, even if we were a neon-blue–colored tribe. To a helicopter flying overhead, it probably looked as if there had been an explosion at the Smurf factory, but damn it, we were united.

Filming didn't begin until after dark, when we became wild natives dancing around a bonfire under the moonlight; by the time the shoot wrapped, it was after midnight. Though we were spitting distance from the Pacific Ocean, there wasn't one single shower available for us to wash off the blue paint. That night, Los Angeles must have looked like "Invasion of the Blue People" as we revved our cars and spread out on the various freeways. I remember watching my speed because, even in Los Angeles, the costume capital of the world, I'd never be able to explain to an officer why I was painted blue. With my teased hair and blue pall, I'm amazed I didn't cause any accidents. I know I got plenty of sidelong stares from other drivers.

When I arrived home, I received an even more puzzled look from my husband, Rolf. The expression on his face was downright wicked! Respect for the sanctity of our marriage prevents me from providing all the steamy details. But I'll just say this: At our place that night, we played a little game of "Earth Man Discovers the Extraordinary Pleasures of Showering with Female Alien."

So why am I telling you all this, aside from the fact that everyone loves behind-the-scenes showbiz stories? The real point, dear friend, is that being overweight does not have to limit your expressiveness in business, or at home. You don't have to be on a TV sitcom or get painted neon blue. Living large can be a fun adventure, brimming with unexpected delights.

2

The Days of Nancy's Life

In 1998, my agent, Marc Chancer, at the Judy Schoen & Associates agency, called to tell me that I had been offered a role on the popular, long-running daytime soap *Days of Our Lives*. A few months earlier, I had met Fran Bascom, the casting director at *Days*, at a party. We chatted and—aware that I was doing film roles in *Speed 2* and *Midnight in the Garden of Good and Evil* as well as various day-player jobs on prime-time TV—she wondered if I would consider doing a soap opera. Some actors have a negative attitude toward daytime television. I don't and I said yes. I thought nothing more about it. So, when the offer came, I was stunned. I didn't even have to audition. But soap operas are set in the land of buff men and petite women. The actresses wear size-two, or smaller, dresses. I'm short and round and I wear a size twenty. I thought the casting director had me confused with somebody else. "No," my agent reassured me, "she knows exactly who you are, and the producers would be thrilled to have you on the show. They have a part in mind that's perfect for you."

Days of Our Lives is set in the fictional town of midwestern Salem, which has seen some extraordinary events even for a soap opera. To give you an idea, for a short time, Satan was a lead character on the show, a favorite female character was buried alive, and a conniving villain committed suicide to frame his love rival for murder.

Though the character I play, Nancy Wesley, isn't "the spawn of Satan," she certainly has her devilish side. She's a sophisticated but sassy doctor's wife with a well-honed manipulative edge. During my first year on the show, Nancy's main goal was to help her ambitious husband, Craig, played by actor Kevin Spirtas, become chief of staff at the local hospital. She was cutthroat and conniving. She did everything from volunteering as a kindhearted candy striper in the hospital to encouraging an unstable nurse to frame Craig's competition with a sexual harassment complaint. I loved her right away, and was able to see her good points, such as her fierce loyalty to her husband. Over time, Nancy has evolved. She is a multidimensional character, containing elements of both pathos and comedy.

I've chosen to play Nancy as a very confident woman, the kind of person I'd like to be around. My personality comes out in her character. Even when we're both scared to death about being rejected, Nancy and I proceed with confidence: We take on the persona of a size two.

During my first two years on *Days of Our Lives*, Nancy's weight was never addressed in the script. Not once. Even when Nancy did hateful, ugly things, the other characters never made a nasty comment about her weight. The folks in Salem weren't in denial about Nancy's size—it's obvious that she's overweight. It just didn't come up in conversation.

Being cast on the show was never contingent upon my weight, or Nancy's, so my contract doesn't stipulate that I maintain a certain size. Nancy's size doesn't serve a function on the show, so why should mine? I can choose to gain weight, or lose it. If someone sees me pick up a doughnut from the snack table on the set, there's no big fuss. But if any of the really trim actors or actresses put on five to fifty pounds, I'll bet it would be an issue. Other actors have told me that they were hired for a specific reason—to fuel the romantic fantasy lives of our viewers.

It's a unique experience, stepping into a character and becoming someone else. When Nancy is evil, it allows me to vent in a way that I wouldn't as myself. Most of us would probably secretly love to take on that outspoken part of Nancy's personality, if only for a moment. Wouldn't it be great to channel Nancy's nasty side and confront a cruel boss, an insensitive lover, or a friend who has betrayed us?

I'm proud to play Nancy mainly because she breaks the stereotype about overweight women. Instead of being a miserable, weak person obsessed with food, Nancy is dynamic, witty, and sexy. Sure, she can be a stinker. It's fun to play. Overweight actresses are usually cast as the downtrodden spouse, ditsy neighbor, or ball-busting wife. In the beginning, the ambitious Nancy was tough on Craig, but the two often shared sweet moments of affection and humor.

When I was cast on *Days of Our Lives*, I had no idea that I would be playing such a powerful, wealthy woman. Details about her were sketchy, which is the way things are usually done on a soap. The writers would rather not commit to a whole preset list of established details when a character is introduced. Instead, they like to be able to add new information and character traits as the story line develops. (Though there have been several occasions on soaps when new information completely contradicts a character's already established history. The creators sometimes feel it's necessary in order to keep the story moving.)

Since the writers usually don't provide an actor with a back story, the actor can take the information that is revealed in scripts and use it to fill in the blanks. It's nothing anyone else needs to know, it simply helps the actor to develop a character. For instance, we learned early on that Nancy comes from wealth. So I decided that she was raised with a sense of entitlement, and understands her power. My own father nicknamed me Queenie because as a kid I behaved like a royal little princess. I projected that particular history of my own life onto Nancy, and then embellished it. Her father treated her royally, I decided, and even spoiled her a bit. I believe Nancy's dad always told her she was wonderful, intelligent and pretty. He was grooming her to take over his business, but instead, she married Craig. Of course, this bothered her father, who didn't think any man was good enough for his daughter. Nancy expects the best, and usually gets it, one way or another. I don't think Nancy has ever bowed to anyone unless she saw it as a means of accomplishing something she desperately wanted.

It makes for a compelling character, which is another reason why I cherish playing Nancy. A fascinating aspect of acting on a soap is that you have leeway in how you play your character; you have room to try different things in your characterization, to add new shadings. When Nancy's ambition was to help Craig get promoted to chief of staff, she was single-minded but she wasn't his puppet. She could be willful and tough on her husband, too. One of her lines was, "I'm calling my daddy to say I'm coming home." Kevin and I decided to develop it as a wicked joke they shared. Rather than use it as a threat to hold over her husband, Nancy would toss it out to lighten the tension. If the directors or producers think you're going over the top, they'll give you a note to make an adjustment. But you have to take chances—an actor's unexpected choices can inspire the writers to add new layers to the character.

Chemistry between actors is a major thing that writers notice immediately. From the first day that Kevin and I worked together, we decided to play Craig and Nancy as a truly happily married couple, and wildly passionate about each other. We thought it would balance the couple's nasty antics. So, even when it wasn't overtly written in the script's dialogue, Kevin and I were physically affectionate toward each other. I'm thrilled that Nancy and Craig are depicted as a married couple in every sense of the word. Our love scenes are written with the same passion any couple on the show enjoys, including the perennial fan favorites, Marlena and John and Bo and Hope.

Actually, my love scenes with Kevin are the only love scenes I've ever played. In my first bedroom scene with Kevin, I was frightened. I wasn't sure what we would be expected to do, or how we would be directed to do it. Kevin was shirtless, and I wore a negligee. In the scene, Craig makes a phone call while Nancy makes the moves on him. I was supposed to reach over and play with his chest.

During taping, I sometimes forget a line; it is something that happens to every actor. But in soaps, we're taping a one-hour show every day. Anyway, my anxiety about that first love scene didn't help. When Kevin finished his phone call, I had a line. Instead, I continued to toy with his very appealing chest. Finally, the director said, "Patrika, it's your line." The crew laughed and we picked up the scene again. Since then, Kevin and I have had several bedroom scenes. We've also been shown frolicking in a hot tub.

Most oversize actresses aren't seen in a romantic way. For instance, on the TV sitcom *Roseanne*, she was always in a flannel nightgown and her husband wore sweatpants. In bed, they talked about making whoopee, and would lunge for one another, but there wasn't any real lovemaking.

Shortly after my arrival on *Days of Our Lives*, Kevin asked me, "Patrika, when the fans ask what you're like, how would you like me to describe you?"

I smiled and answered, "Kevin, I can't tell you how to describe me. How you see me is how you should describe me."

"How *would* you describe yourself?" he quizzed.

"I'm a short, round, redheaded woman."

Kevin has told me that fans, many of them large women them-selves, have approached him and asked, "How can you be with that fat woman?" His response has always been, "You're talking about the wonderful lady who plays my wife." Kevin says he realized that the heavier female fans were often looking for some sort of confirmation that he cares about me off-screen as well. It was a projection of their own insecurities; if this gorgeous hunk could care about his over-weight costar, then maybe they could find people in their own lives to value them, too. I was touched that Kevin connected with the fans on such a profound level; he's a sensitive and honest guy, and I'm honored that he's my costar and friend.

Although I was the Tetley tea lady in TV commercials for nine years, and have appeared in several films and television programs, I'm usually recognized in public because of Nancy on *Days of Our Lives*. For most people I meet, I'm sort of a safety net. Since I smile a lot, I give off positive and peaceful energy that helps someone to feel safe around me. I also think fans feel comfortable approaching me because I'm familiar in the sense that I'm overweight (like many of them); therefore, I'm considered less than perfect—even flawed—just as they might see themselves. I'm accessible, and I'm greeted as if I was some-one's kindergarten teacher, or a former coworker.

One day while Rolf and I were walking the dog, we stopped to buy coffee and pick up the new soap magazines. I was standing out-side holding the dog while Rolf ran into the store. Nearby, a heavy-set girl struggled with a newspaper machine. She rattled the machine and I asked, "Do you need some help?" Without looking up, she answered, "No, thanks. The machine's not working." She started to walk away, then turned and looked at me; she recognized me, hesitated for a second, and came walking back. "I'm new here, and people in Los Angeles probably don't say this much, and I'm probably not supposed to do this," she blurted out, "but I just love you! I can't believe you talked to me!" She recognized me from my films *Daddy's Dyin' . . . Who's Got the Will?* and *Leaving Normal*, as well as the sitcom *Step By Step*. After we talked, she promised to start watching *Days*. Whether they recognize me from my work on *Days*, commercials, or films, the encounters are always nice. It's as if I have a million friends all across the world.

When I make a personal appearance at a soap event, the fans usually respond to me differently than they do to the other cast members. With the guys, the screaming women see them as sex symbols; they want to touch them, and tear the shirts off their buff bodies. But when I'm introduced, the audience sees me as their sister, mother, or best friend. We chat about the different stars I've worked with, and where I buy my clothes. Fashionwise, I'm likely to wear blue jeans or my black jeans by Cherokee—an affordable line for larger women available at Target. I want to be dressed neatly and nicely but comfortably, since I'll be sitting signing autographs all day. We do the "girl talk" thing. They ask me: Where do I buy my clothes? How does Rolf feel about my bed scenes and kissing Kevin? How do I handle people who bug me about my weight? Does Rolf complain about my weight? And they often ask me how I'm treated by other actors. I think that last question—especially if the fan is overweight—is really a way of getting an indication as to how she might be treated by other actors. Usually, there are a few people who don't know me, but they figure, "Hey, she's a Hollywood actress. I'll get her autograph, anyway." Soon after, I'll get a letter that begins with, "I met you in Duluth. I never watched the show, now I tune in regularly. I was really surprised by how much I love it."

The comment I most often hear is: "You're so much smaller in person!" I love hearing it, but there's a reason why I seem smaller in person. The TV cameras, with those wide-angle lenses, make me look a lot bigger on-screen, especially when I was wearing that unflattering red-and-white candy-striper's costume that accentuated my size. At the studio, we called it the Buick. As my character evolved and developed, I was eased out of the candy-striper uniform. Finally, one of the wardrobe people said, "I think you're out of the Buick for good." Now as the chief of staff's wife, Nancy wears very stylish clothes and does fund-raising rather than candy-striper–level volunteer work.

I look forward to hanging out with my fans at soap opera events, and I like talking with fans who recognize me when I'm out in public. I enjoy making time for them. Some soap stars I know—who shall remain nameless—won't give their fans the time of day. I'm talking about stars who have been on a show for more than ten years, and who could give a rat's ass about their fans. It's unfortunate and sad. I've been on the show for four years and I hope I never get to the point where I'm tired of my fans. In defense of some of my coworkers, it's true that some of them have been threatened and stalked by so-called fans. With that kind of experience, it's not surprising that they want a little distance and might seem aloof sometimes. Generally, however, our fans are a support system, almost like a family, offering love and encouragement. I'm grateful for their support and their expressions of friendship. Because the fans (and producers and coworkers, too) tell me I'm doing a good job, it's given me the confidence to persevere— without fans, I probably wouldn't be where I am today. Every vote of confidence I get from my fans makes me stronger and more determined to be successful in a field in which I shouldn't be—by stereotypical Hollywood standards.

After a public appearance, fans will approach me and say, "You're so funny. You should do stand-up comedy." It's something friends and coworkers have told me all my life. Years ago, I even gave it a shot. I was successful at it, but I absolutely hated doing it.

When you're onstage performing stand-up, it's just you and the audience; there's no script, no character to hide behind, no other actors to share the stage, no props to keep you busy. It's as if you're standing completely naked in front of a crowd of strangers and asking,

"So, what do you think?" In addition to feeling so vulnerable, I hated the clubs—smoky rooms filled with drunks. To overcome my discomfort and downright stage fright in that situation, I used to psyche myself up by pretending to be a character. It didn't help. I couldn't get past hearing the emcee introduce me as Patrika Darbo. As a security blanket, I'd invite all of my friends to come and watch me, but when I looked out at the audience and saw half of my address book sitting there, the last thing I felt was secure. I was too preoccupied with wondering, "What are they thinking?" If a joke didn't go over with the audience, I was embarrassed for them to hear it.

When I'm playing a character, it's okay if people don't like it. But in stand-up, if the audience doesn't like what they hear, or see, then it's me they don't like. I have great admiration for stand-up comedians; it takes a lot of courage to get up there. But I'm more comfortable letting a character such as Nancy bear the brunt of that type of rejection. I'd rather have the applause and fan support. I guess that's the people pleaser in me.

After I had been on *Days* for a little over a year, it was revealed that Nancy had had a baby girl she had been forced to give up for adoption. As a teenager, Nancy was raped by a friend of her father and became pregnant. The little girl was raised in an orphanage outside Salem. In 1999, Nancy and her daughter, Chloe, now sixteen, were reunited.

When Chloe, played by Nadia Bjorlin, arrived in Salem, she only wore black, her hair hung straight, and her glasses were unbecoming. Her attitude was off-putting and aloof. At school, Chloe was often teased for being "different." I envy a character like Chloe because even though the taunting from other students causes her pain, Chloe sticks to what she believes is right for her. But there's a big difference between being flexible with your appearance and giving up important values. The only person who's always going to be here to take care of you is you. You can sit back and look at a situation. You can analyze it and then determine what the best thing to do is, so you don't hurt yourself or someone else, and then move forward to attain your goal.

During my third year on *Days of Our Lives*, an overweight teen, Susan, was introduced. She was a shy classmate whom Chloe befriended. Weight was an issue for Susan. She felt ostracized by the other students because of her size. To gain confidence and win acceptance, Susan tried dieting. This was the story line that led to Nancy's size being addressed for the first time.

Nancy, who can be a control freak, wasn't pleased that Chloe had bonded with someone who was also an outsider at school; she feared that the friendship would only make her daughter more isolated and alienated than she already was at that time. Susan sensed Nancy's disapproval and it created tension between them. In one scene, Nancy asked the shy teen, "How is your diet going? It looks like you've lost a few pounds." The teen shot back, "Why are you interested? Thinking about joining me now?" When Nancy explained that she was only trying to make conversation, Susan remarked, "It seems like somebody who is so comfortable with herself is pretty obsessed about weight."

Personally, I felt awkward about how the scenes between Nancy and Susan might be interpreted by viewers. My main concern was that an overweight teen watching at home might think Nancy was unnecessarily cruel to Susan simply because she was heavy. In my performance, I tried to emphasize that Nancy was being protective of her daughter, and that it wasn't Susan's weight that troubled Nancy, it was her outsider status. Chloe was already an outsider, and bonding with another outsider would only make it more difficult for Chloe to be popular—something Nancy felt was important for her daughter. In time, Susan emerged from her shell and made friends at school without losing weight.

Women of size are usually supporting actors and only the "perfect" women are leading ladies. Even though it's an unwritten rule, it's still sexist. On *Days of Our Lives*, for many years Joseph Mascolo, who played Stefano DiMera, was a large man. He's not built like the physically fit Drake Hogestyn, who plays John Black. Yet Stefano was a leading character and had no problem getting women to fall for him. Face it: On most TV shows and in films, the man might not even be close to Adonis, but his wife, or girlfriend, is always a ten, or at least a nine.

Camryn Manheim won a Golden Globe and an Emmy for her work on the courtroom drama *The Practice*. Did we see any new larger women on her show or elsewhere? No. I won a *Soap Opera Digest* Award and was nominated for an Emmy. Have soaps included a greater variety of size among women? No. Prime-time shows feature several overweight actresses, but are they strong leading women? No. Change, if it comes at all, comes ever so slowly. Sexism. Sizeism. Sexism. Sizeism.

I love *Days of Our Lives* and everyone who's involved with the show. But the truth is, men run the show, from top to bottom. From the majority of the crew to the executives at NBC, there are men everywhere. So it should be no surprise that, even on *Days*, much of what Nancy does is move her husband ahead in his career. She became a volunteer and made her way around the hospital, keeping tabs on everything that was going on. In that way, Nancy and I are alike, but our motives are very different. How many times did I volunteer to do things in school? I served refreshments, handed out fliers, decorated the gym. I was included in events even if I didn't have a date, and it wasn't a bad deal. It got me off the sofa and out of the house so that I could meet people and make friends.

The desire to be liked, and wanting to fit in, often makes heavy people try to please everyone, and I'm no exception to that; I have a hard time saying no, and I've put up with a lot of garbage just to fit into whatever group is hip at the moment. It began in high school, and still lingers today, though I'm now conscious of my behavior and can choose to take a different course.

Nancy may not have been the queen of her prom, but she was probably in the queen's court. She and Craig probably danced all night long. Me? I didn't go to the prom. Still, I fit in somewhere because I needed to be liked, and I made the effort to participate in groups. I may not have had a boyfriend, but I had friends.

In 1999, *TV Guide* teamed up with *Entertainment Tonight* to come up with the "Sixteen Sexiest People on Television." There were two soap opera personalities among the ranks, a man and a woman. Of all the lithe and lovely soap actresses, they chose me! I was one of TV's sexiest actresses, alongside some of the most beautiful young faces in television: Alyssa Milano (Phoebe Halliwell on *Charmed*), Lara Flynn Boyle (ADA Helen Gamble on *The Practice*), and Tangi Miller (Elena Tyler on *Felicity*). Of course, it was an honor. Hey, they touted their lineup as having "that certain special something that makes us irresistible." But when you've grown up insecure, there's a curious thing about achieving success and recognition, whether it's in show business or any other walk of life. Though we know we've earned the success, we still have trouble accepting it. There's the shadow of our former self, and all the negative forces we've previously faced, taunting us to diminish the achievement. I could have cued the old mental tapes still stored in the dark recesses of my mind: my aunt telling me, "You can't be an actress! You're overweight. You'll never be anything!" Or my mother telling me I couldn't sing. Neither woman knew what they were talking about. Luckily, their words only made me more determined to meet the goals I'd set for myself. Today, I have supportive people, like Rolf and Kevin, around me. Kevin often encourages me to accept compliments with a simple "Thank you," and to remind myself that I deserve them.

So, fortunately, I had the presence of mind to enjoy every single moment of my triumph in *TV Guide*. When people complimented me, I chose to accept their kind words with grace. Hey, why shouldn't I? I'm one of the sexiest people on TV!

PART II
Getting Personal

3

The Cuts and Scrapes
of Childhood

If my mother had to pass a parenting test before I was born—
and I was her first—I wouldn't be here today. (I know, who
doesn't feel that way?) Oh, she did the best she could. I don't
believe she ever did anything deliberately to hurt me or my
younger siblings. If anything, she made quite a few personal sacri-
fices to provide for us. The adult me understands this, but the child
in me still hasn't come to terms with growing up.

Just about everything that makes us who we are starts with family. As children, we first define ourselves by how our parents see us,
how they relate to us. The lessons that we learn—positive or negative—stay with us through adulthood. Our parents were influenced
by their own childhoods, just as their parents were. Each generation
informs the next; maybe that's why there's so much dysfunction in
the world. Unless we learn from history, we are bound to repeat it.

One way to break a negative family pattern is through rigorous self-examination, challenging the concepts we learned in childhood and questioning whether they're appropriate for the person we are today.

My mother always believed her own parents favored her brother. They showered him with attention and spoke glowingly of his achievements. She, on the other hand, could do no right. Of her two parents, Grandma Esther seemed to be the most disapproving. Personally, I'm convinced she was just plain jealous of her daughter because of the different path my mom took in life.

Grandma felt pressured into marriage by her sister, my great-aunt Minnie, and her sister-in-law, Grace, who were both already wed. Their attitude seemed to be, "Come on in, the water's fine!" Easy for them to say; they were both newlyweds, happily floating in the shallow end of the matrimony pool, still too young and inexperienced to comprehend the dangers that awaited them in deeper waters.

Eventually, Grandma caved in to the pressure. She gave up her independent lifestyle and job as an English teacher in Washington, D.C., returned to Wisconsin, changed her religion, and married dear old Grandpa Tom in 1920. In time, she learned that he could be stubbornly provincial in his narrow-mindedness (in those days, it was called traditional). Yet she remained by his side for four decades, quietly resigned to that one particular line in the wedding vows, "till death do us part."

In contrast, my mother made the most of her single years. Unlike Grandma, she subscribed to the philosophy, "I'm going to do it until I get it right," which led to her first marriage to a hypnotist, then a second to a restaurant owner, and then a third to a baseball publicist who was a dwarf. During, and in between, marriages, she lived all over America. She sang popular music of the time at local clubs like Borcellino's in Cleveland and as a backup singer in music studios. Later, she worked in restaurants and baby-sat for Perry Como's son. She wasn't skilled, but she enjoyed working at different jobs. Grandma must have seethed, stuck in a rocking chair next to her old coot of a husband, thinking of the bountiful banquet of life experiences my mother enjoyed.

Today, I suspect that my mother has always been jealous of me. I have the career she once dreamed of but never quite achieved, working in show business. No doubt, she would have kept pushing, trying to make her dream a reality, but getting pregnant with me pushed her into a second marriage, which led to more children. I know she was unhappy staying at home and caring for three kids. Meanwhile, I enjoy a level of freedom she barely got to taste, primarily because of my conscious decision not to have children. My mother's resentment of me mirrors the resentment Grandma felt for her and allowed the cycle of dysfunction to continue.

After I was born, Mom got pregnant again, and I got a baby sister, Peggy. We're only eleven months apart, so I don't have any cute tales about treating my adorable little baby sis "like a dolly" and I don't remember her birth. I do remember that we constantly fought for our parents' attention, like most siblings do, especially when they're born so close together. Our baby brother, Danny, joined us eighteen months later.

I think raising three small children contributed to the stress between my mother and father, but there were other reasons for their marriage being, ultimately, doomed. Let's just say they were incompatible. When they finally filed for divorce, it was hard on all of us. I was five years old.

Soon after the divorce, when I was in second grade, Dad remarried and we gained a stepmommy. At the time, we lived in Plant City, Florida, with my paternal grandmother. Dad and his new wife found a place in nearby Jacksonville. My sister and I were already in school, unlike Danny, who was only three. It was decided that he would live with Dad and his new wife, and we'd visit them on the

weekends. The transformation in towheaded Danny was remark-
able. Suddenly, he was the little prince, as if he were an only child.
On our weekend visits, Danny enjoyed taking Peggy and me by the
hand and leading us to his room, where he would show us all his
new toys. There wasn't a bare spot on the floor; we'd have to climb
over the old toys just to see the new ones. He had become the apple
of our dad's eye. My sister and I hated him for it.

Meanwhile, with stepparents in the picture, our little family
was growing by leaps and bounds. Mom had met hubby number
three, Don. He was four feet, two inches, a midget. My new stepdad was known as the biggest little man in baseball. He'd been
with the Milwaukee Braves ever since they were first in Boston. As
a kid, he was an unofficial mascot—a handicapped kid whom they
favored and who seemed to bring them good luck—for the
Boston Red Sox. He had also been a bat boy and knew Babe Ruth
and other baseball greats. While in college, he was a performer
with the Roller Vanities and was quite successful, and after graduation from Boston College he joined the Braves's organization and
stayed with them right through their move to Atlanta. He worked
in publicity as the traveling secretary and assistant to the chairman
of the board. After he left the Braves, he had the same position
with the Houston Astros. He had been told that someone his size
couldn't do the job and he proved them wrong. I admired his
determination.

Shortly after mom's third marriage, she began to feel run-down.
At first, she assumed it was a flu that she couldn't shake. She felt
feverish, her muscles ached, and she experienced severe headaches.
The symptoms didn't clear up, and she visited the doctor. And then
another. And another. With each new doctor, the tension mounted.
With each new doctor, there was a new diagnosis, and new rounds
of tests. She was poked with needles, prodded with strange-looking
instruments. She received advice—get more rest, change her diet,

get more exercise. One disease after another was ruled out, each more horrifying than the last.

Finally, she received a diagnosis. Mom had lupus, an autoimmune disease that can affect virtually any system in the body. Think of it as a "self-allergy" in which the body attacks its own cells and tissues, causing inflammation, pain, and possible organ damage.

She was immediately put on a regimen of potent medications, including steroids.

While she was struggling to deal with the fact that she had this disease, Mom had gotten legal custody of us. She made arrangements to have us come live with her and Dad in Milwaukee. I was still a kid; I didn't fully understand what the heck was going on, why there was suddenly so much confusion.

For most people, growing up with your parents is the natural order of things. The thought of being raised by anyone else is incomprehensible. It wasn't that way for Peggy, Danny, and me. We spent a lot of time with our dad but he didn't have custody and had to return us to Grandma until Mom picked us up. Grandma Williams, my biological dad's mom, was a loving, nurturing parent figure. She'd bake chocolate chip cookies, and we'd climb up on stools and stand by her side at the kitchen table licking the spoons and bowls. If we scraped a knee while playing in the yard, she'd gently apply a Band-Aid and say just the right words to make us feel better. At night, if we were frightened by crashing thunderclouds, she'd let us curl up in bed next to her. With Grandma Williams close by, the scary shadows in the far-reaching dark corners seemed less frightening. Living with her was really the only stability we experienced, and now we were being uprooted.

Saying good-bye to Grandma Williams was excruciating. We were moving to another part of the country. Mom reassured us that we would visit Grandma Williams, but we didn't believe her. For all we knew, Wisconsin was a million miles away from Florida. Our stepdad was on the road with the Braves, so our mom's brother, Uncle Tommy, and his wife, Aunt Eve, picked us up. Peggy, Danny, and I sat with our faces glued to the car's rear window, screaming, "I love you, Grandma!" while she stood in the middle of the street, a smile frozen on her face as she waved good-bye. Grandma Williams put up a brave front, but we knew the separation was hard on her, too. Gradually, she faded from our vision and disappeared. We were on our way to a new life, with Grandma Williams left behind. I've often wondered how she coped in the hours after our departure. Did she cry, or keep herself busy with housework? Did she make dinner that night as usual, or simply retire to bed early? Even years later, I never asked her. But the image of her standing stoically, a solitary figure in the middle of the street, remains frozen in my mind.

Since we didn't know the real reason for the move to Milwaukee, we thought Mom was being selfish and reckless. To us, it was as if she'd awakened one morning with the bright idea that she suddenly wanted to play mommy. I can still clearly remember, as we left Jacksonville, driving past a pet store. In the window, we could see the adorable tiny puppies and kittens playing in their cages. Peggy and I looked at each other, both with the same thought: If Mom wanted someone to take care of, why couldn't she have just adopted a pet?

After we arrived in Wisconsin, I can't say that things settled down. Living with lupus is a daily challenge and some days Mom felt fine, other days she could barely get out of bed. Meanwhile, her mood careened like a roller coaster without brakes, climbing, teetering, up, and then soaring down. Back then, I don't think that most doctors considered the emotional side effects of the drugs they prescribed and their adult patients didn't know any better either.

Without an explanation for Mom's wild mood swings, we came to the conclusion that everything was, basically, our fault. How could it not be? One day, we were her darling little angels, and then the next, we were her worst nightmare. So I grew up walking on eggshells, wondering, "Who am I today? Am I good, or bad?" It wasn't an environment that built self-esteem and confidence, but it sure made me attentive to every minor change in the emotional atmosphere. I became a master at adapting my behavior. When a twitch in Mom's eye indicated imminent anger, I'd try to ward it off by heading for the kitchen, where I'd quickly pour another cup of strong black coffee for her, struggling to keep my hands steady so I wouldn't drop the pot or cup and, inadvertently, unleash a maelstrom of outrage from Mom, whose ears were keenly tuned to the slightest creaking of a floorboard.

If one of us did something wrong, and didn't confess to our crime, my mother would warn, "If the guilty one doesn't fess up, I am going to spank all three of you." That way, she knew the right one would get punished. But if someone stepped forward and admitted guilt, no one would get a spanking. So, to avoid the spankings, I'd single myself out as the guilty party even when Peggy or Danny had been the actual wrongdoer.

Taking the bullet had its downside. Often, a little time would pass after the incident and then Peggy would go to our mother and quietly identify herself as the real culprit. The outcome? I'd get spanked for lying. This went on from the time I was about five until I was nine or ten.

My mother felt pride in being a tough taskmaster, someone who doled out spankings without remorse. When I was in my early forties, we had an argument about it. Mom boasted that she always knew who was really guilty. "Then why did you threaten to spank all three of us? You were encouraging me to be a liar," I told her. "What kid wants to be spanked for something they didn't do?"

Growing up, I began to figure out that I had choices. I could sit at home in the tiny world of our household and wait for the ax to fall on my head, or I could get out and meet other people. Everyone needs to be around people they like and have that feeling returned. Sometimes, it takes effort to find those people; I made it a personal mission. I'd volunteer for extracurricular activities; at lunchtime, I joined different clusters of students at the various school cafeteria tables. I circulated, and learned about the activities they enjoyed. If it appealed to me, I'd join, too. My original intent was to find my own group, peers who would immediately make me feel accepted, but, gradually, I discovered I could be part of many groups. I became the wild card, the free space on a bingo card. To this day, I can get along with people just about anywhere. Whether fitting in was a learned behavior or an innate ability, I don't know. But I'm grateful for it.

In contrast, my younger sister, Peggy, found her crowd right away: the tough kids. You know the ones: They skulked around the far-off corners of the schoolyard clad in black and smoking cigarettes. People who know Peggy and me have always commented on the fact that we're as different as night and day. It was especially glaring during our adolescence. I was Miss Congeniality, whipping up fudge brownies for a bake sale or hanging the homecoming banners, while Peggy was the rebel chick without a cause. When she walked down the school corridors, crowds would part, clearing a wide path for her and the bad attitude she carried with her. Surprisingly, Peggy's reputation as a tough kid had an upside. I was able to bask in her ill-repute, her notoriety. Wherever I went, students would whisper, "That's Peggy's sister. Leave her alone, don't make trouble."

The only person who *did* make trouble for me was Peggy. She was one of those people who, if she suspected the slightest weight gain, would swear off food. So, while Peggy was busy starving, she'd taunt me about the food on my plate, calling me a "big fat slob" nearly to death.

She hated the way I looked. One day, when we were in our late teens, I had come home from painting theater scenery all day. I was a messy, dirty, tired-looking "big fat slob." She was upstairs, getting ready for a blind date. When the boy arrived before she came down, I rushed to the door and said, "Hi, I'm Peggy. Sorry, I'm not quite ready." It was a payback moment that could've been better if she hadn't come downstairs before he bolted.

The move to Milwaukee was tough on all of us, but I think it was hardest on Danny. He lost his coveted position as "the only child." Instead, he was now one of three kids. People didn't cater to him; he didn't get his own way. My brother, who was extremely bright, reacted by standing out at school. He'd play the class clown, cutting up and making jokes, entertaining his classmates and infuriating his teachers. Because he was academically ahead of the other students, school bored him. Coming on as Chuckles the Clown stimulated him and got him attention.

The three of us did have our bonding moments. Once, while we were riding home on the school bus, a group of tenth-grade bullies picked on Danny, who was then in the sixth grade. Even though the bullies were two grades ahead of me, I scrambled out of my seat to protect Danny. Peggy, who was in seventh grade, did likewise. I whacked one on the head with my purse. Peggy balled up her fists and tore into the mob. "Leave our brother alone!" we wailed. The bullies backed off. When we got off the bus, the three of us walked home, heads held high. Later, we teasingly gave Danny a hard time for nearly getting us pummeled by a bunch of tenth-grade bullies.

What parents say to their children obviously has a profound effect on how they develop as people and my upbringing was no exception to that. For example, I have a terrible time singing. Growing up, if my mother heard me singing along with the radio, she'd shout, "Shut up, you can't sing." Imagine my surprise when I was cast in a musical at school. During rehearsals, the music teacher would look at me and say, "Great! Wonderful!" But in my head, her words of encouragement were drowned out by the sound of my mother screaming, "Shut up, you can't sing!"

As I mentioned, my mother was at one point a professional singer, but it fell by the wayside when she became a mom. At parties, when I was very young, someone would invariably play the piano while my mother charmed the guests, performing their favorite tunes. Eventually, she lost interest in being the designated party entertainer. I think the enthusiastic applause became too painful for her, serving only to remind her of what she might have been. About the time she realized that she was not going to be the next Rosemary Clooney, I took an interest in singing myself, the sounds of my cheerful "the hills are alive with the sound of music!" echoing throughout the house. I'll bet Mom wanted to exile *me* to the Swiss Alps.

Just as words from a parent can affect you, so can a nickname they give you, even though it might seem harmless. My biological father nicknamed me Queenie. He thought that, even as a toddler, I talked, and acted, like royalty. What he meant by that, I don't know, but I had a title better than some little princess. In fact, Queenie was the only name I went by until I started school. Then, my kindergarten teacher decided Patsy was a better fit. She might have thought it was a simple shortening of my name, but for me it was a little more sinister. With one fell swoop, I went from royalty to just cute little Patsy, and it was a name that made me think of someone who was easily duped or victimized. To this day, I cringe when I hear the name Patsy. (A sincere apology to all of you kind, loving Patsys out there. It is just a personal association thing for me. I hold no judgment against you.) Thankfully, I was called Queenie first, so I built up an attitude of expecting to get what I wanted (with plenty of hard work), and I didn't (usually) allow myself to be treated badly. Had I been called Patsy from the start, I might have hung my head in perpetual cute-nickname victimhood for the rest of my life.

Meanwhile, Dad stuck Peggy with the dubious nickname Muttsy. It was meant with love, but he took great pleasure in explaining to people that, the first time he looked at Peggy, he commented, "What an ugly little mutt." Peggy was in her thirties before she finally shook the terrible tag. Even today, Dad's widow still calls her Muttsy.

Like any children, we believed whatever came out of the mouths of our parents, or, for that matter, from any adult. Positive reinforcement is great, but it seems as if the negative barbs are nearly impossible to shake. At the most inopportune times, I can still hear my mother saying, "You're not worth it; you're fat!" I still hear that echo in my head when people congratulate me on my Emmy nomination, or when I was about to go onstage to sing in *Bottom's Up*, and even today when I sing at events and shows with my *Days* castmate Kevin.

In time, my mother—who died in 2001—regained her strength and partially recovered. She always had lupus, but her medications became more advanced and she improved. But it's taken me a lifetime to overcome the emotional bruises experienced in childhood. I still have my moments. But I believe it's necessary to face your demons and come to terms with your past, even if it's one step at a time. Do that and you build a foundation for creating the life you were meant to enjoy.

4

My Day Job

An actress, especially an aspiring one, never knows when the call will come. Many years ago, when I was in my Los Angeles apartment watching television, the phone rang. At eight o'clock in the evening, the last thing I expected was an audition call, but when I picked up the phone, it was a casting assistant who introduced herself, apologized for calling at the last minute, and asked, "Are you available for work tomorrow?"

I didn't hesitate for a second. As if I had been practicing for this all my life, I blurted out, with no thought of how I would get time off from my day job as a credit manager at Panasonic, "Oh, sure I am!"

"Great," she replied. She gave me the directions to the Sunset-Gower Studios, in Hollywood, where the auditions were held for *The Jeffersons*. She wanted me to arrive dressed in shorts and a tank-top running outfit. I was trying out for the role of a marathon runner.

Marathon runner? Her words brought images of skin and bones, running and sweating. As I wrote down the directions, I wondered how she'd gotten my name and phone number. At the time, I didn't have an agent. But I was registered in the *Players Directory*, a catalog of actors used by casting directors. I realized that my picture in the *Players Directory* was only a head shot, so I was quite certain when I heard "marathon runner" that someone had made a terrible mistake. Before she could hang up, I said, "We haven't met before, and I don't think you know me."

Confused, she responded, "Well, no. We haven't met. But—"

"I would really love this job," I explained, interrupting her, "but I'm an overweight woman and I don't think that anyone looking at me would classify me as a marathon runner."

"Oh, well, oh, ah, well, hon, I really appreciate your telling me that," she fumbled. "Thank you so very much. I'll keep you in mind for something else. Good luck."

I thanked her for thinking of me and said good-bye. Simply a harmless mistake, I figured, and I didn't give it another thought.

An hour later, the phone rang again.

"Patrika." I instantly recognized the voice. It was the casting assistant who had called earlier. "They want you to try out for the part."

She had spoken with the producer and found out that they wanted someone *exactly* "my type." She told me to come in for the audition the next morning.

"As I mentioned earlier, wear a runner's outfit. If you get the part, you'll be working all day and into the evening."

At midnight, I was still tearing through my drawers and closets, looking for anything that could pass as a running outfit. A woman my size doesn't usually have cute running shorts and a cute top in her wardrobe, and I sure didn't. Meanwhile, I had to figure out something to tell my boss. I decided to use the good old standby we've all used at one time or another. I said that I had to go to the dentist. A crown had come off, and it needed to be fixed; after the dentist, I'd head directly for the office.

It was after midnight before I was able to go to bed satisfied that I had come up with clothes that would work. In a corner of my closet, I found a pair of shortie pajamas that I had made for myself. They were bright orange. I used navy blue hemming tape to edge the sleeves and the neck. I had designed it to sleep in, but with the clock ticking, I decided it was good enough to pass for a tank top and shorts.

I didn't want to attract unnecessary attention in my orange jammies/running outfit, so I wore them under a conservative skirt and blouse. I also wanted to be prepared in case I didn't get the part and had to go to my regular job.

I called the office and told my fib about the loose crown. I sensed suspicion on the other end of the line, but I was running late and didn't have time to deal with it. In the car, I rationalized that it was probably just my own guilt echoing back at me.

I arrived at the casting office and saw five overweight women seated in the reception area. They were also contenders for "overweight marathon runner." I noticed an assortment of odd ripples; like me, they wore their workout clothes under regular outfits, probably because they also had day jobs they needed to get to if they didn't get the part. We had all called our offices, willing to skip out on our bread-and-butter jobs because we wanted to act. An hour passed with no sign of the producers. It was making all of us wanna-be actresses very anxious; everyone checked their watches and tapped their fingers. The producers arrived and apologized for being late, explaining that they hadn't realized the auditions were today. Their performance wasn't very convincing. But our gracious, fake responses were worthy of Emmys.

Movies and television have tried to capture the stomach-churning stress of auditioning for a part. In the dramatized version, the would-be actor's behavior is usually heightened to show nervousness and apprehension. In the real-life version, there's no time for such spotlight emoting. Basically, we were called into a room, one at a time, and the producers stared at us. I smiled pleasantly. Meanwhile, my insecure mind raced with the harsh judgments I imagined they were having about me. I did my best to block them. I had to appear relaxed, calm and cool. When it appeared that my moment was about to pass, I blurted out, "Don't you wanna see my shorts?"

That got their attention. Their stunned expressions seemed to say, "She talks?" Two male producers chimed in unison, "Excuse me?"

"You guys made me get out this outfit, and now you don't want to see my shorts?"

"Yeah, okay," one of the grim-faced producers volleyed back, "we want to see the shorts."

Without missing a beat, I hiked my skirt *over* my head and announced, with my face covered, "These are my shorts!"

I didn't wait to see their reaction. I simply lowered and smoothed my skirt, said "Thank you," and exited with dignity. I felt great because I knew that if I didn't get this job, they'd remember me for another because I could tell they liked my spunk.

Before I could make my way outdoors, the casting director chased after me. "Wait, you can't go anywhere!" she commanded breathlessly. "The producers have to make their decision. If you get the role, you have to stay and work."

I rejoined the other contenders in the reception area, where we silently sat, waiting for the gods to reach their verdict. Every few minutes, the monotony was broken by the sudden appearance of the producers, who stood and stared at us. Each time, they whispered back and forth. Finally, one of them said, "Darbo, you got it."

I didn't allow myself the luxury of feeling excited; there was no time to bask in my good fortune. I was too busy freaking out about how to tell my boss that one emergency dentist appointment had just turned into several sick days. After thanking the producers, I asked to use a phone. "The crown needs extensive work," I mumbled, trying to approximate the voice of someone with a mouth numbed by novocaine. "And there's another tooth that needs a root canal. I'm in severe pain and won't be coming in today." Or tomorrow, or the next day: There were rehearsals and finally the day of taping.

Taping the show was a blast. In this episode of *The Jeffersons*, George was running in a marathon, but he was so out of shape that a handicapped man, an overweight woman, and an extremely elderly man could outrun him. Whenever the episode is repeated, I get mail from *Days of Our Lives* viewers who caught it. Ah, the magic of television.

Before I could support myself full-time as an actress, I spent seventeen long years as a credit manager with several types of businesses: mobile home financing, the music industry, the medical field, and the computer world. In the nine-to-five world, I learned that a lot of employers believe overweight people don't deserve to have the better-paying jobs. Their preconceived notion is that we cannot control what we eat, so how can we possibly be put in charge of anything that requires discipline, focus, and detail? We are often put in the back room, away from view, where we are given as much work as we can possibly handle, and then some. Heavy people don't complain as much, if at all, because we've been made to feel we should be grateful that someone's given us a job. We often don't make waves, even while doing the most amount of work for the least recognition.

Curiously, I noticed that overweight male employees had a better shot at being promoted to the coveted higher-paying positions. Big physical stature in a man implies—often without basis—strength, power, and solidity. Large men, even those great big teddy bears, generally have less trouble landing dates than big women, who, incidentally, can be just as smart, savvy, and sexy. Some people need a little social reeducation. That's tough to do when the misconceptions are constantly reinforced by film, television, billboards, and print ads. But despite all of those barriers, it ultimately comes down to each individual overweight woman to define how she will be treated by the world.

I believe that had I been a man, there would have been no question I would have been promoted. But not only was I a woman, I was overweight. At the time, I carried two hundred pounds on my five-foot, three-inch frame. In business, a woman's weight and physical appearance continue to play a factor when an employer decides which candidate he wants to hire. We are less than perfect if we are not an average size. There are men, and some women, too, who believe that a heavy woman is not taking care of herself. Therefore, they feel they don't have to care either. They take it as permission to chip away at the overweight woman's self-esteem. Frankly, I accepted that cruel behavior for far too many years. To compensate, I exhausted myself trying to please and prove myself.

The pattern began in high school, when I got a part-time job at a five-and-dime. In one corner of the store, there was a tiny coffee shop. It had three booths and a counter with eight stools. I was the original multitask worker: waitress, short-order cook, busperson, and dishwasher all rolled into one. At inventory time, I counted the stock. During college breaks, I'd return to my job at the five-and-dime. I was a dedicated, reliable, personable, full-service employee.

After college, I was employed by a bank to do credit investigating. I worked credit checks all day. Then I went to work for a company that financed mobile homes and did both credit investigations and collections for them.

I was always very good at my job. There were mobile home dealers who warned their prospective buyers not to give me more than one-word answers, and to respond only to the questions I asked. The dealers wanted to sell those tornado magnets as fast as they could. They also knew that I could get more information out of a person than most others. I was really good at skip-tracing, too.

I'd get a little piece of information and be able to track people down. I had a knack for getting people to the phone, too. I was better at it than many other collection agents. I played cute, coy, downtrodden, sultry, or mysterious to get someone to take my call. Once I got them on the line, I'd turn into the bill collector and demand payment.

For example, in a sweet, girlish voice, I would say, to whoever answered the phone, "Oh, phooey, I really, really need to speak with him. Is there any way you could help me? This is my first week and if my boss finds out that I can't . . ." Before I could complete the sentence, I'd have my sought-after deadbeat on the line.

I also flirted in more direct ways. I'd ask whoever answered the phone, "How are you doing today, sir?" I'd wait for his response, and then I'd fake a stutter, as if I was blown away by the mere sound of his voice. "Oh, I'm sorry, sir," I'd stammer. "Have we met before? Your voice, it just sounds so familiar." We'd go back and forth before I'd finally say, "Can I ask your roommate a quick question?" Within moments, I'd have the delinquent debtor on the line. So it wasn't the greatest job, but to this day, I'm grateful for it because it helped me to develop invaluable acting skills. I learned to catch people off balance, the same technique I applied at that audition for *The Jeffersons*. It's a given that in our often competitive society, women try harder, and overweight women have to try even harder.

Doing most of my work over the phone provided me with a mask to hide behind, and anytime we don't have to be seen, we're far less self-conscious and a broader range of personality emerges. That's especially true of anyone with the least bit of shame or concern about his or her appearance, whether it's size, hair loss, a visible scar, or a physical disability.

Do you realize that many of the women who get paid to work the phone sex lines are my size? I know several plus-size actresses who do it to earn the rent. It's an opportunity for an overweight woman to vent sexy feelings that she might not have the chance to express in her real life. Over the phone, she becomes what other people want her to be. The telephone allows her to pretend.

While working the phones at the credit agencies was different than a phone sex line, there were similarities. With the buffer of the phone, I came alive; I could be anyone I wanted to be. Men flirted with me and I flirted back. I never had to lie about how I looked because it didn't come up. Conversation on the phone would be lighthearted and lively, but once we met in person, sometimes the good cheer evaporated. I never dated anyone I met through business phone conversations, but we would sometimes cross paths in the course of company functions. The reality of who I was didn't live up to the idealized image they had already created about who they thought I was—or thought themselves to be. Quite often, they were not what they portrayed themselves as being on the phone. It was always interesting—and sometimes irritating—to watch their faces in that first moment that we'd meet. I was the same person; I hadn't changed. I still related to them in the same way. But when they saw me, sometimes their attitude toward me changed. If I didn't fit the picture they had conjured up in their minds, I was a disappointment. It's unfair, but that's life. I'm not responsible for someone else's mis-conception or fantasy regarding what they think I look like. I have to say, too, that sometimes it was a great relief for both of us to dis-cover we were not the Adonis and Athena we might have imagined each other to be. There were nice, friendly moments like that, too.

Acting involves a good deal of fantasy, and it was always a won-derful escape for me as a kid. I think we all manage to find good things about ourselves and circumstances that we can hide behind. When I was a schoolgirl, and I heard a cute guy call me a fat slob, it hurt. But in spite of my weight, when I was onstage in school plays, as far as I was concerned, he—and everyone else—would love me. Talent is attractive. So is self-confidence.

Even the most well-intentioned coworkers can overstep boundaries without giving it a second thought. There's plenty of emotional sabotage that accompanies sharing a doughnut, even if it is
unintended. "Patrika, you've been so good on your diet," a coworker
would coo. "You can have half a doughnut." They didn't always
realize the ripple effect that can happen by breaking a diet with a
smidgen of doughnut. Sometimes they did but did not care because
of their own issues and insecurities. Before day's end, I'd find myself
in the gift store, buying a candy bar. On the way home, I'd think,
"Oh, you already broke your diet. Call today a loss. Pick up some
ice cream and start again tomorrow."

I remember at one job, instead of dieting by only cutting down
on food, I tried to eat more healthily. I paid strict attention to what
I ate, and was feeling really good. Sure, I'd still get cravings for
French fries and cookies, but they would pass.

One afternoon, I went to lunch with a colleague and commented, "Veggies are great, but right about now, I sure would love
some cheesy, gooey lasagna." It was an attempt to start a conversation and turned out to be an ill-fated one.

"No, no!" he snapped, pointing his fork in my face. "*You* can't!"

I felt like a bad little girl getting scolded by a parent. Sure, I
would've liked some lasagna, but I had no intention of ordering it
that afternoon. Even if I had, what business was it of his? Why
couldn't he have said, "Yeah, me, too. I love lasagna," or, "My mom
makes the best lasagna!" Anything but "No!" What if he mentioned
it to our boss later? Would it send the message that I wasn't self-
disciplined? And as if feeling insecure wasn't enough, I even
thought of asking my lunch companion, "Are you going to like me
less if I stop dieting?" Unfortunately, at that point in my life, I
hadn't developed the skill of being so forthright and direct out
loud, but I did have the sense to realize that I wasn't at fault. This
guy was unbelievably body-conscious, so it was his problem, not

mine. Being able to distinguish between what is someone else's issue and what pertains to you is important; it contributes to peace of mind and helps to keep you balanced. I make my own food and lifestyle choices. No one else does. It's important for me to let people know how their words have affected me. I've learned to stand up for myself and speak up. If I don't, the feelings I don't express will fester and I might go home and eat a gallon of ice cream.

This kind of behavior among my colleagues added to my frustration about being overlooked for job promotions. I purchased a popular book, *The Sensuous Woman*, the semiscandalous bestseller by "J." I hoped some of the tips in it would help my career advancement. I followed some of the advice; I purchased contact lenses. I lost seventy pounds. I'd been a jellyfish for long enough! The inequity finally angered me into taking action that went beyond the superficial change in my appearance. With the help of an attorney recommended by the National Organization for Women, I filed a discrimination lawsuit, charging that I wasn't receiving equal pay for equal work. I won the suit, in an out-of-court settlement, but lost the war. I was sworn to secrecy about the conditions of the settlement. I was also given the option of continuing in the company, but with a condition: To maintain my position, I'd have to relocate to a branch office in another state. The company knew that I had recently gotten married, and was interested in acting, and that I couldn't leave Los Angeles. So I had to resign. I stood up for myself, but I was also jobless. It's the price you sometimes pay for having the courage of your convictions.

I took the first credit job I could find, one in the medical industry. It was pretty much like my prior position: I collected money, investigated credit, and reconciled accounts receivable. But I was miserable working in hospital billing, a field that I knew very little about.

Eight months later, I returned to the music business, but it was more of the same. I was in a familiar rut, doing the work but getting neither the appropriate pay nor the recognition. Still, I stayed with it for three years while acting on the side. After eight months, two of my immediate supervisors quit, and I was left with a workload that had been handled by three people. I'm proud to say that I rose to the occasion. Sure, I felt overwhelmed sometimes, but the main point was that I could successfully do the job. Eventually, I felt I had demonstrated my ability to handle responsibility in a multitask environment. So I asked for a raise. I thought I deserved it, and figured the company would see it the same way. Instead, I was informed that I wasn't up to the task. They brought in another person to handle the job, and to add insult to injury, I had to train my new boss. That was it. I marched into the vice president's office and said, "You teach him! I quit!"

I ended up getting a job as a waitress; I was happy because the schedule was flexible, allowing me to pursue acting gigs. I had worked as a waitress for two weeks when I was cast in a road-tour company of *Bottoms Up*. It paid more than the waitress job, and I was valued as an entertainer, which was my primary goal.

Eighteen months later, the tour ended and I returned home to Rolf. He had been laid off from his job as a producer at Disney in 1982 during a management change, and that meant I needed steady employment. I was soon rehired in the collection department of the music company I had left. It led to a small, but well-timed, victory.

I was working at the same level I had had before I left the company, but the position involved a lot of grunt work and they soon wanted me to oversee another area. I told my boss that if I was going to do that, then I wanted to be a manager. I also wanted the title, the salary, and everything else that went with it. They gave it to me.

WHEN YOU WALK INTO ANY ROOM, THE INITIAL IMPRESSION you deliver determines 75 percent of what people will think of you. An overweight woman has two strikes against her: gender and size, both qualities that are overlooked in overweight men, who are more often judged on their résumés alone. I think that's because many male bosses think of their staff as their own personal harem, where every female subordinate reflects their image. Female bosses realize what a challenge it is to get to the top, and often will not tolerate anything around them but perfection in aptitude as well as appearance. Again, it's a reflection of their power image. Sometimes, sadly, women can be even harder on other women than men can be.

Learning all of this meant learning to play office politics. Sometimes, that meant letting the men I worked with think they would be getting something more than business from me. I wouldn't flirt, or ask for attention. But I didn't react with offense to their advances. I also noticed that, when I lost weight, men suddenly became more physical. The "buddy" arm around the shoulders came with a new little squeeze, or a slow stroke down my back. At times, it was downright scary; I was surprised by the liberties men would take and would even experience guilt, wondering what I had done to make them think I would welcome their advances. When did being slender become a signal for a willingness to play sex games? Some of the women I worked with also changed their attitude toward me. One day I was a pal, and then, seemingly overnight, I was considered the competition even though I was happily married. Since I believed it was all part of playing the game, I said nothing, and I thought I had learned to play the game very well. It seemed as if I was in control, but since I was not being true to myself, I really was not in control at all. I felt compromised by justifying my acceptance of inappropriate behavior. I finally realized that in the corporate world, management always takes care of management, and it was up to me, the individual, to take care of myself. I refused to sabotage my personal and professional growth for the sake of pleasing others.

Meanwhile, I was still doing theater and auditioning for commercials and other acting jobs. I managed to go to auditions on lunch hours, or I would have another one of those "dentist" or "doctor" appointments. If I got an acting job that would last a day or two, I used my vacation or sick time. I came to hate my day job, but I needed it. In the music business, there were a lot of loud, obnoxious musicians and drug abuse. But I overlooked the dark side because I was playing the game; I could get through it without making waves.

My department got a new top supervisor who behaved like— and strongly resembled—Jabba the Hutt from *Star Wars*. He told me that my "acting thing" didn't fit the company's corporate image and offered me a twelve-dollar-per-week raise if I promised to give up my acting aspirations. I quit. I understood and respected his concerns, but you have to learn to create boundaries and then stick to them. It also forced me to learn what my priorities were. Sure, I needed money and benefits, but I realized that this or any job wasn't worth sacrificing my dreams.

Fortunately, I was doing much better as an actress. I was getting more roles, and felt something more permanent was just around the corner; I was gaining more confidence, and was daring in the risks that I took. Leaving my job in the music business was a huge risk, especially since I had had an offer for a substantial raise, but I knew I wouldn't go anywhere in the company, so I was glad to leave. The trick was to see that even though being let go from a job might seem like a door was being slammed in my face, it was really somebody opening one for me.

Although I was making more money acting part-time in commercials for Tetley tea and Herfy's Hefty hamburgers, and on episodes of *St. Elsewhere, Bay City Blues, Gimme a Break,* and *Growing Pains*, I still needed a full-time job that included some sense of security. I found another credit job, this time with a computer company. But after a few months, it fell into serious financial trouble. The vice president of finance who had hired me was dismissed, and a new one was hired to replace him. At a management meeting, the information I gave at a presentation contradicted what the new VP had said. Although I did it within the context of a report, in a businesslike and polite manner, he took me to task over it after the meeting. We were in the hallway. He towered over me, his big, ugly finger in my face, spitting that I should never contradict him in a meeting.

"What do you know, anyway?" he fumed. "You're just a woman. No better than a goat! Don't ever contradict me again."

I summoned all the techniques I had learned from acting classes, inhaled deeply, and yelled as loudly as I could, "Bah, bah-ye!" Everyone in their offices stopped working and peeked out their doors. All they saw was me strutting down the hall and my boss about to blow another gasket. It was one of the best days of my life. Within the year, I was earning more money as an actress than my former boss, who, for all I knew, was still stuck in corporate hell.

Aside from my business sense and acting talent, I think I've gotten work in the corporate world, and in show business, because I do get along with a broad spectrum of diverse people. I'm an absolute professional. I believe many women of size possess the ability to look beyond the cover, making us richer as individuals because we are more apt to talk to people who are not considered typically attractive. We know what it's like to be judged only by our appearance. It can help us to develop empathy and therefore be more open. I'm grateful for that kind of wisdom, and I'm thankful for having learned when it is right to stand my ground, without malice or offense. Whether I'm coming, or going, I've learned how to strut with confidence and I love it!

5

Love and Marriage

y relationship with my husband, Rolf, began as a backstage romance. We met working in a community the-
ater production of *Anything Goes* in 1971. Rolf was a stage manager
and I was in the chorus. During rehearsals, I noticed Rolf watching
me. Under any other circumstance, I would've thought, "Oh, this
guy's attracted to me." But my actress insecurities overpowered my
womanly instincts. I thought he was preoccupied with me because
I was doing something wrong onstage. Finally, during one rehearsal,
I caught his eye and he gave me a goofy smile. My heart raced.

Shortly after, we both went out for coffee with a group of the
actors. Rolf gave me his complete and undivided attention. He
asked me why I was drawn to acting, where I grew up, things that
showed he took an interest. I was also fascinated, listening to Rolf
talk about his life. We immediately felt comfortable with each other.

During this particular production, I was responsible for a prop.
One night, during a performance, Rolf barged into the dressing
room in a panic. I was talking to some of the other actresses, in my

underwear, with my costume over my head, when I heard Rolf
sputter something about a prop problem. There I stood, half naked,
my dress not quite over my head. While peeking through the neck,
I told him it was on the prop table where it belonged.

That night, after the show was over, I was heading for my car. All
of a sudden, Rolf raced out of the building waving a pair of panty
hose in his hand. "Are these yours?" he asked, stopping me dead in
my tracks. Lo and behold, they did belong to me. Without realizing
it, I had dropped them as I walked across the stage to the exit. Just
like he had misplaced a prop earlier, I had lost something of mine. As
I accepted the panty hose, Rolf asked if we could go out that
Saturday night. My jaw dropped. In the course of a few hours, he
had seen me half naked, chased me down with my panty hose, and
now, he was interested in going out with me. Well, how can you say
no to a guy who just held your lost panty hose in his hand? I smiled
sweetly at him and answered, "Yes." Of course, on the drive home, I
reviewed the events of the night and wondered to myself, "Just what
kind of girl does he think I am? Does he think that just because I
was loose with my panty hose, I might be the same way on a date?"

We went to a party at a friend's house. It was November 11,
1971. I ended up staying the night at Rolf's. We had such a good
time that neither of us wanted to end the date. Before you jump to
any conclusions, we didn't have sex. Instead, we cuddled in his bean-
bag chair and fell asleep listening to Broadway show-tune albums.

That doesn't mean Rolf didn't make any moves. Trust me, on
that first date there was some very heavy petting. I remember feeling worried about what he thought of me because I had allowed
things to go so far so soon. I later learned that at that same time,
Rolf was saying to himself, "This is great! I'm glad she's not one of
those girls who's worried about what I think of her." I'm glad I
didn't play coy, and say anything about it out loud. Who knows? We
might not have continued dating!

We spent Sunday visiting the La Brea tar pits, an archaeological site and museum in the middle of Los Angeles, walking around the park together. It was a beautiful, sunny day. That night, I went home. On Monday, I told everyone at work that Rolf was the man I was going to marry. I had no idea why, except that it was instant love. We were fortunate that we had the theater in common. It was a great springboard for learning about other interests that we also shared.

When I started dating Rolf, I was probably fifty pounds lighter than I am now, but since then he has been with me through every diet, up and down. I know it drives him crazy because he worries about my health. I've had to tell him to stay out of my eating habits and take care of his own. Rolf doesn't take care of himself very well. I think he likes it when I diet because it forces him to become a better eater, too. Overall, we respect each other's choices about food and keeping fit.

Rolf was my first true love, and turned out to be my first heart-break. After we'd been dating awhile, I inadvertently made a discovery about Rolf's past. We were on an afternoon date, a bicycle-riding outing with the Mickey Mouse Recreation Club, Rolf's Disney employee group. At that time, I weighed about one hundred and forty-five pounds. My hair was in pigtails, and I was wearing pants that were a little too big for me. There we were, pedaling along together, when Rolf pointed to a woman who was wearing a little hot-pants outfit and said casually, "Oh, there's my ex-wife." My heart stopped. And then things went from bad to worse.

I couldn't keep my bike in gear. It toppled over, followed by me. It could've been a skit on *Rowen & Martin's Laugh-In*. Except, instead of Ruth Buzzi or Arte Johnson toppling over, I was. As you might suspect, the mishap did nothing to improve my mood. The only thing worse would have been actually being introduced to her.

Rolf took me home. We were standing at the door when he said, "I hope seeing my ex-wife didn't upset you." It was an opportunity to address what I was feeling, but before I could answer, Rolf added, "I never said anything before because I didn't think that you would care." In a way, I was touched that he thought I'd be so accepting, but it also hurt me that he thought I wouldn't care. There was an awkward silence. We said good night and Rolf left. I cried all night long. We've all been there, right? Half a gallon of ice cream, a package of Oreos, a box of Kleenex at hand. The ugly cry, sniffles and all.

Finally, I called Rolf the next day at work and said that we needed to talk. At dinner the next night, I told him, "Please don't ever tell me you didn't think I would care." Without realizing it, he had really hurt me by assuming that. An ex-wife I can handle, but not communicating, that was my biggest issue. Rolf explained that when we'd met, he was going through his divorce. So he had walls up that I didn't even know about. I soon learned, brick by brick, what they were.

One problem with Rolf having an ex-wife was that he kept mistaking me for her. Being a Southern gal, I was ready to marry early on, but Rolf didn't feel that way. He was afraid we'd repeat the same mistakes they'd made in his first marriage. I tried to be patient. But we had our share of flare-ups because I somehow felt that I was a stand-in for his ex-wife; he was transferring the problems they had onto our relationship. Because I felt Rolf was closing off and was afraid of getting too close, I resented the fact that their crummy marriage created distance between us. Sometimes I get frustrated and tend to lash out at the person I love.

To work out the issues of closeness in our relationship, we enrolled in a class based on the book *Open Marriage* by Nana and George O'Neill. Although the book talked about open marriage in the sexual sense, too, Rolf and I agreed that we wanted to be sexually exclusive. Like the book, the course we took had a lot to offer about openness in communication (even making appointments to

discuss things that became issues) and pursuing individual interests—
like parties, concerts, classes, and friends—without each other. The
instructor was a psychologist, a Dr. Elsie King. She urged me to get
out of the future and start living for the here and now. Elsie said,
"When Rolf's ready to get married, he'll get married again. And if
you're not willing to wait, then move on. Don't keep pushing him."
She wanted Rolf to get out of the past, and stressed that I wasn't his
ex-wife.

I took the class to show Rolf my willingness to invest in our
relationship. I realized he had been hurt by his first marriage and
didn't want either of us to be hurt. He never knew his wife was
unhappy until the day she'd asked for a divorce, so communication
has been a big lesson for us. I felt I did everything possible, but I
remember one argument, when I told him, "You put one more
brick in the wall you're building between us and I am gone." Either
Elsie never mentioned anything in class about giving ultimatums,
or my head was somewhere in the clouds. But trust me: Issuing
ultimatums serves no purpose unless you're willing to face the consequences. There's pushing, and then there's shoving.

So we went through the open marriage stuff. That summer, we
also built sets together for the company's theater productions.
Painting backgrounds for the plays allowed us to spend time
together working and talking. Without realizing it, we were living a
metaphor; we were also building a solid foundation for a strong
future together.

Two years later, in November 1973, Rolf and I were sitting
backstage during a production of *Arsenic and Old Lace*. He casually
looked at me and said, "You know, we've been seeing an awful lot
of each other. I think we ought to make it permanent." In
December, we wed.

Friends have since asked me, "Do you ever wish Rolf's propos-
al had been more romantic?" I suppose it would've been nice. But I

knew going in to our marriage that Rolf didn't have a romantic bone in his body. He makes up for it in other ways; he is calm, warm, and consistent, and I don't need any surprises. There is enough drama in my life without having to worry about the stability of my relationship. Rolf provides me with that stability.

Six months before we got married, Rolf and I had taken a trip to Canada. Half the time, we were Mr. and Mrs. Davidson (my maiden name), and the other half of the time we were Mr. and Mrs. Darbo. Money was tight, so we split everything fifty-fifty. Rolf and I thought of it as our first honeymoon.

Shortly after the wedding, Rolf and I went to Hawaii. A baseball meeting was being held there, and my stepdad had arranged discounted rooms for us. We flew on the Los Angeles Dodgers plane. It was a nice gesture that came from out of the blue. So our second honeymoon—the official one—was inexpensive and loads of fun.

Rolf had met my dad when he'd come to Los Angeles for a ball game and later met my mother when she came out with Dad on another occasion. But the first time he got the full picture was when we went to visit my sister, brother-in-law, and brother in the south. I think it was probably for the best that we were already man and wife. When he finally met my family, he couldn't chicken out about marrying me.

I nearly met Rolf's mother, sister, and brother while looking like a hooker. Rolf is an amateur photographer and wanted to take some fun photos of me at military post signs on the way up Route 101 to Camarillo. For the photos, I put on a silver lamé gown and a silver wig and lots of makeup, including big false eyelashes, but instead of doing the camera work on the way up, I insisted on wearing and being introduced in normal clothes. We took the photos on the way home.

Though I tease Rolf that he's not a romantic, he insists otherwise. Still, I can count on one hand how many times, in nearly thirty years of marriage, he's given me flowers, and he has never given me candy. But as we approach our thirtieth anniversary, in 2003, I can say that Rolf has total, unconditional love for me. He gets on my nerves sometimes, and I know I get on his. There are times when I want to bite his head off, and he's felt the same about me. But we've learned how to get along.

There was a time when I was working at a job that I hated; any job that wasn't acting, I hated. Meanwhile, Rolf was unemployed, at home and not looking for work. I was touring in *Bottoms Up*, singing, dancing, and doing comedy skits. Every single week, I sent my paycheck home. When the tour was over, Rolf was on my case about getting another job. It was a tense time, and there was a lot of anger between us. Had we not been married as long as we had, we might very well have gotten a divorce. If I had just come off working four days straight on a show, and the tomatoes needed to be watered, and it was my day to do it, then I needed to stop what I was doing—whether learning lines or just watching TV—and water them. End of discussion. He wouldn't get up to do it for me.

Obviously, you can tell our marriage isn't perfect. But what real-life marriage is perfect? Regardless of the problems we encounter, big or small, Rolf knows that I love him, and I know that he loves me.

When Rolf and I married, he became my family. An unfortunate family disagreement between my sister, my mother, and me caused a rift with my blood family. They tried to come between my husband and me. I understand the concept that blood is thicker than water, but when you enter into a marriage, I believe you become one with your spouse. It's as close as you can get. Husbands forget that their wives take precedence over their mothers. Mothers often forget this, too. When a wife doesn't take precedence, problems in the marriage start. I have now been with Rolf longer than I was with my own family. Rolf and I are Darbos together, so, if there is a choice between my family or my husband, I choose my husband.

There are many people out there who believe that people should get married primarily to procreate. If a couple doesn't want to procreate, they are treated as abnormal. So many people have asked me why I got married if I didn't plan to have kids. Hello? Because I wanted to be married to my husband, not my kids! That's why. I had to deal with judgment about not wanting kids when Rolf and I first got married. My mother always regretted that she had kids when she was young. My sister said she didn't want to follow in her footsteps, but she did, and when I comment that she did things just like Mom, she protests.

As for me, I've chosen not to have kids because I am selfish; I realize it and I admit it. Plain and simple. If I were in a position to choose between buying a diamond ring or buying the children new shoes, I wouldn't trust myself to make the right decision. Beyond mere selfishness, though, there's another reason that I don't trust myself to raise children. I believe that you treat kids the same way you were treated as a child, and I'm not ready to face that risk. I love my nieces and nephews. I lavish them with gifts and enjoy being around them. But at the end of the day, I can say good-bye, so I feel I have the best of both worlds.

I think the "gotta-have-kids" feeling is outdated, an almost puritanical kind of thinking, and still, a bunch of old men continue to tell us women what we're supposed to do. It's hammered into us from childhood, and there are far too many women who still believe it. Sex is only for procreation? Ha! Have children, or don't, but there's no reason to confuse sexual pleasure with sin and obligation—and never forget that the choice is yours.

I don't need to give Rolf children to prove that I love him. In fact, without children, we have the time, money, and energy to do things together that nurture our relationship. We go out more often because we don't have to hire a baby-sitter, we travel together, we take classes, we enjoy the theater—all without depriving kids of something they would need. We enjoy our lifestyle. Our marriage resonates in a special way because we're devoted to each other and we've even developed our own "love language."

We have our own little thing with each other called spoon. When we say, "Spoon," our lips go into a pucker, like a kiss. No matter where we are, we can say "Spoon," and know we're sending a personal message, a kiss, to the other. At home, if one of us says, "Spoon," the other comes running. We always kiss each other good-bye and good night. In fact, spooning is probably our favorite thing to do. A friend of mine, Pamela, and her husband use the word "forty" because she used to draw a kiss under every fortieth thing on her "honey-do" list for him. Now they use "Forty!" as their secret kiss message.

Kissing is probably the most intimate act shared between two people. Remember the Julia Roberts and Richard Gere movie *Pretty Woman*? She was a prostitute, and he was the john paying for her services. She wouldn't allow him to kiss her on the lips. Kissing was something that was too intimate to barter for cold cash. It wasn't until after they fell in love that a kiss was exchanged.

Of course, there are other ways to kiss. For instance, you can kiss parts of your lover's body: his ear, the nape of his neck, his hard . . . forehead. But, ultimately, nothing tops a soulful lip kiss. Wonderful things happen when lips meet and a curious tongue begins to explore. When Rolf and I kiss, the next thing I know, we're nibbling each other as our hands caress each other's body. Kissing leads to exploration, and beyond. It's the journey to the beyond that is always fun.

I have had fantasies about having an affair. One time, my friend Noreen went to a cast party with me. There was a man who took one look at me and my knees turned to Jell-O. Later, we talked and I grew more attracted to him. Noreen joked that she was going to have to find another ride home and worried about what she would tell Rolf when I didn't come home.

I couldn't tell you what it was about the guy at the party that got me so worked up, because he wasn't that attractive. But if he had touched me, I might have responded, "Okay, where are we going?" It scared me that I was so transfixed by him; if Noreen hadn't been with me, I could have found myself in serious trouble. This happened six, or seven, years into my marriage, so it wasn't as if Rolf and I were newlyweds. But ever since, if Rolf doesn't accompany me, I don't go to parties without having somebody by my side. That encounter was so unsettling, such a brush with temptation, that I never want it to happen again.

An affair is arranged, and planned, with skulduggery. It's cheating. In contrast, an encounter has a surprise impact on your brain cells, chemistry that just happens. I didn't avoid an affair with the gentleman at the party; I wasn't interested in planning for one to happen. What I avoided was that chemistry with someone other than my husband. It was from out of the blue, a gift that I could enjoy on its own terms for the moment. I am glad I was saved from trying to take it further because I might not be where I am at this moment in my marriage, or in my life. I might be in a whole different place; but I made a decision not to take that road.

I have wondered if opportunity was knocking on the door, offering me a better life than the one I already had. Could this man have been the "something better just around the corner" that some people use to prevent themselves from committing to a relationship? These fleeting thoughts occasionally visit my mind, as they probably do for all of us. So, you see, my fantasies aren't necessarily sexual. In fact, I probably have more fantasies about being taken away from worldly concerns like paying bills. I fantasize about being totally worshiped and supported; every day I could shop until I dropped!

Finances have torn the best marriages apart. It's an area in which communication can play an important role. If one of us wants to make a purchase that's more than a thousand dollars, we discuss it. But if I want to splurge on a two-hundred-dollar pair of designer shoes, there's no discussion. I love not having to ask for permission. If I have to ask permission, then I have to ask myself, "Why?"

Having taken the open marriage course, the first thing I would tell young couples is that marriage is not a fifty-fifty proposition. It is a 100 percent and 100 percent proposition. If either one of you has to give up 50 percent of yourself, then you are not entering into the relationship whole. Sit back and talk about the fact that you like this and he doesn't like that. He is not going to learn to like it just because you want him to. It used to amaze me in college when I heard my girlfriends discuss their boyfriends. They'd describe their shortcomings and confide, "When we get married, I am going to change all that." I never understood that. Find someone you already like just the way they are.

Based on my childhood, I don't have a strong background in marriages that work. My mom divorced twice. My dad married several times. For a period, I was raised by my grandparents, who stayed married for better or worse. I think what's helped me is a willingness to bring who I am to the marriage, and accept Rolf for who he is, and then have the willingness as equal partners to work on keeping our marriage strong. I also think second marriages are best. I'll remind Rolf of this every now and then to keep him on his toes. Ours is his second marriage, but my first.

I've written that Rolf and I are opposites in nearly every way. But opposites attract, right? Sometimes, I wish Rolf were more flexible about trying new things. But it passes. If he changes his ways, fine; if not, that's fine, too. The reward we get from our marriage is that it's open. Neither is forced, or expected, to do what we don't want to do. There are no restrictions. Rolf is a member of several different organizations that hold little interest for me. When we married, I didn't expect him to give up his interests, nor did he expect it of me. If there's a lecture, or a movie, that he wants to go to and I'm not interested, he goes. So regardless of how different we are, we respect the difference, while also finding things that we can do together.

It's fascinating to me that some women I know won't even show their bare, make-up-free faces to their own husbands, morning or night. If I had a long night, and nothing's planned for the next day, the last thing I want to think about is getting up and putting on makeup. Some wives can't fart in front of their husbands. What is that about? They can do all kinds of intimate things together, but when it comes to passing gas, they have to flee the room. It's ridiculous!

Rolf has taught me to appreciate that love truly is blind. When my weight goes up fifty, or sixty, pounds, he looks at me in the same way he did when we got married twenty-nine years ago, when I weighed a few pounds less. I also look past the fact that he has gotten older and gained a belly. Rolf is also my business manager. I am his employer and his partner in life. But regardless of the changes in our relationship, or marriage, I still see my husband as my "Rolfie boy." So love is blind to all faults and roles. We have time invested in this relationship. We can both say we are together because we want to be together.

Rolf and I laugh a lot. I think it contributes to a good marriage, and a happy life. When people look at us, they can't believe we're older than they think. I remind them that we don't have children, and aren't as stressed out because of it. They usually respond, "Oh, right," as if they know the secret, too.

Communication is everything in marriage. To this day, Rolf and I make it a point to discuss anything that upsets either of us. So, even though it's far from the perfect marriage, we have one that's worked for us for twenty-nine years, and continues to be strong. I have been asked, "For God's sake, after twenty-nine years, what the hell do you two have to talk about? My answer: "Everything!"

PART III

Between Us Women

6

The Masters Must Know

Ooh-la-la, ladies, we just love those European men. Going to Italy and having our fannies pinched gently as the gorgeous Italian shocks us with the naked longing and admiration in his eyes is fun. Going to France and having our hand held by an exciting Parisian as he slowly lowers his lips, touching it with the tip of his tongue and never breaking the spell of his eyes locked with ours is delicious. Going to Greece knowing that our every fantasy can be fulfilled by those beautiful dark-skinned Mediterranean men is exciting.

Wouldn't it be great if we could send all our American men to Europe to take a course on "Romancing a Woman"? Once they received a passing grade, our studious guys could progress to the advanced class, "Everlasting Pleasure." Of course, we'd have Pablo, or Pierre, teach our boys the things about women they grew up learning from the world around them. These European men have dedicated countless hours to gazing at sculptures in parks, paintings in their world-renowned museums, and art, in of all places, their metro stations. What were they looking at most? Women. Art is filled with big, beautiful, voluptuous women. Meanwhile, our cowboys have been staring at the boob tube, and those skinny twigs with silicone breasts on *Baywatch* are not even in the same world as the beautiful figures seen in the Rubenesque form worshiped by classical artists.

Titian's *Venus of Urbino* is the perfect example of beauty, form, shape, and size. In this painting, Venus is the epitome of sensual delight as she languishes on slightly mussed sheets. Clearly an openly sexual woman, she is posed as if beckoning her lover to come closer. Her arm is stretched partially over her rounded tummy, and her hand is lying over her womanhood. Is she hiding, perhaps? Or maybe even "caught in a private act," if you know what I mean. The flowers in her other hand lets us know that she is ready to blossom into a woman, and maybe even to unfold her petals in a garden of sensual delight.

Lara Johnson, a plus-size supermodel, recently posed for a picture in the style of Titian's ideal woman. I was so glad to see a renewed appreciation for the classic ideals of womanhood, beauty, and admiration. Forget about posing like some cheap hoochie. Why not imitate the classic beauty that highlights our figures the best? We can drape a sheet where we want to hide something, and let it fall open where we want to reveal. Can you imagine a waif striking a similar pose? No way! Why? What is so sexy about these classic images is their full-figured bodies. I can't really explain why, but there's something so sensual and liberating in their naked poses that it seems only right that we, with our rounded, soft figures, should be the models. Step aside, Cindy Crawford, we're moving in.

We just need a chance to show the world beauty again in a way that reveres the female form rather than exploits it. The painter

Sandro Botticelli met Simonetta Vespucci and couldn't take his eyes off her. He ended up spending the rest of his career painting her as his Madonnas or Venuses. He was captivated by her curves, and red lips, as was the rest of the male population in Florence. By holding herself with confidence, sexuality, and sensuality, Simonetta made all the men crazy. You can tell by the look in Simonetta's eyes that she understood her destiny to rule the world of beauty and art as Botticelli's muse. Simonetta also knew that, without her, the poor guy didn't have a chance of succeeding on his own.

The Baroque artist Peter Paul Rubens also used voluptuous and round figures to portray women the way he saw them: robust and beautiful. At that time, being a plump woman meant you were rich and could afford plenty of food; you were part of the elite. The men of that period seemed to be fascinated by the curvy shape of a woman's body. Today, we're made to believe our guys only desire a female body as shapeless as that of a ten-year-old boy.

In Rubens's *The Garden of Love*, all of the female models are double, if not triple, chinned; flushed pink in the cheeks; and have overflowing breasts that spill out of their dresses. Stop by your local bookstore and look for the painting in an art book. Pay close attention to the beguiling look in their eyes. Their demeanor doesn't suggest that they think no one wants them. Quite the opposite. They're posing as if the entire world wants to hold them in their arms, and these juicy beauties get to pick the winner. As the women lie around the garden, seducing their favorite suitor, they seem to admire each other's bodies as several legs and arms are intertwined, in waiting. You get a sense that ten minutes after the modeling session ended, a mad orgy erupted.

Spain, too, was a country that adored round women. Francisco Goya painted *Portrait of Doña Isabel Cobos de Porcel* and had no idea, as he stroked the canvas, that this would be his most famous piece. Goya's model was eventually considered to be the "embodiment of womanhood," not only because of the way she looked, but because of the way she lived. Doña Isabel loved food, and people around her connected the sensual act of eating with being as gorgeous as she was. Her hands were plump, and her chins layered, but her most famous piece of anatomy was her butt. It was said to rival the biggest of them all, which gave her the reputation as the most wanted woman in Spain.

The *Portrait of Madame Barbe de Rimsky-Korsakov*, by Franz Xaver Winterhalter, is a famous painting of the biggest party animal of her day. She had an unstoppable appetite, and fed it at all hours of the day and night. Within years, madame gained enough weight that it was more than obvious to her partying buddies. You're probably thinking that she freaked out and went on a crash diet, right? Wrong. She was proud of her new size, and became more desirable with each added pound. The additional weight didn't stop her from being beautiful, confident, and dramatic. If you get a chance, take a look at this piece, and then check out Chrissie Marie Crawford, a big, beautiful model, in her "madame" pose. You'll be amazed by the resemblance and the shared beauty.

Though the art I've described is tasteful and restrained in showing the female form, not all artists were as conventional and puritanical in their sensibilities. Manet's *Luncheon on the Grass* is set in a park, with a naked woman entertaining two well-dressed men. The woman is clearly comfortable with her size, and her nakedness, because she's showing off her big thighs and overflowing breasts. There's no doubt about it: She's seducing both of them. Believe it or not, even the Parisians found those sexual overtones too much. Some people of the time thought that the model was supposed to be a prostitute, but my eyes tell me something different. I see a gorgeous woman sitting next to a picnic basket with two rich men. She's got food and she's got a choice of men . . . or both, if she'd like. I'd say that's not a bad situation for any woman.

Renoir was another shocker of his time. He was an Impressionist who loved the female form. He is reported to have remarked that he wasn't finished with a painting until he felt that he could pinch the canvas. That's my kind of guy, because I've got plenty to pinch.

A discussion about art would not be complete without mentioning Picasso, one of my favorites. One of his most enduring paintings is *Women Running on the Beach*. In it, two naked women run along the shoreline in total freedom. They are clearly having a great time with each other. It's no mistake that Picasso didn't set a man in the painting. To me, this shows that Picasso felt women could be all things he loved about them: sensual, free, sexy, and naked, without the presence of a man. Works for me.

The more I study art from these periods, the more comfortable I am in associating beauty with my shape. It's not that I ever thought my shape was ugly. It's just that society's narrow standards shook my confidence. I started to believe that I was wrong and that the media was right: Skinny was good and big was bad. Now, I have such an appreciation for beauty and art that it makes me feel powerful, confident, and sensual. Ladies, get a print or a poster of one of these paintings and hang it in your bedroom. I guarantee you'll see beauty in a way you probably never conceived of before.

7

Feeling Good Naked

Toddlers are almost never self-conscious about being buck naked. Still dripping wet from a bath, they can scurry through a house faster than a greased pig. By the age of four or so, we are typically taught modesty; we develop a sense of privacy about our bodies. Of course, that's also about the same time boys and girls begin playing doctor, young children exploring the fascinating differences in each other's bodies. Often, a parent happens upon this completely innocent scene; how that parent reacts has a profound effect on the child's future attitude about sexuality. Sadly, far too many parents teach their children shame.

A different kind of shame is taught to children who grow up carrying extra pounds, particularly girls. I can't remember ever feeling good about seeing myself naked when I was young. My sister was the tormentor and taunted me mercilessly about my size, the portions of food on my plate, and what I put in my mouth.

Meanwhile, my svelte sister obsessed about her weight, and constantly put herself on crash diets. I realized that she was struggling with her own issues about food (her svelte days are long gone). But it didn't stop me from feeling pain. To avoid the hurt, I comforted myself with more food.

Well-meaning teachers sweetly commented, "You have such a pretty face. Think how much more beautiful you'd look if you controlled your appetite." Parents chastised us about our appetites, and insensitive classmates held us up to ridicule: All these contributed to the sense of shame we developed early on about our physical appearance.

We got messages from the outside world, too. In the late sixties, the English teen model Twiggy was the standard of beauty for my generation. Her name tells you everything you need to know about her size. And movies, television, the beauty magazines we read, all reinforced the message, "If you're not thin, you're not worthy." Ironically, the same media that told me I wasn't worthy also sent a mixed message. There was one aspect of my ample body that had value: my boobs. The sly, panting looks I caught from teenage boys told me that I could make them quiver with desire. A hard-core feminist might call that objectifying. I saw it as a lifeline to building self-esteem. As I got older, I enjoyed standing in front of a mirror, my top off, turning and admiring my boobs from different angles. I also noticed that my curves were pretty shapely.

And try wrapping this idea around your mind: While we are hiding at home, swearing that we'll start our diets in the morning, there is undoubtedly someone out there who wants us lying down, flat on our backs, ready to do the nasty. If we don't get out and play the game, we'll miss the delightful opportunities that await us. While you're sitting in front of the tube, snacking on pizza and ice cream, I can guarantee you one thing: Prince Charming will not pop out of your closet (unless it's the platonic male buddy you're secretly drooling over, the one who dropped by with the ice cream, and *The Sound of Music* on VHS). There are available men who adore big women, so get out there and hunt them down. Bring one home, and let him make you feel sexy. A friend of mine, who's also plus-size, tells me she's met some fascinating fellows in Internet chat rooms. Who knows? Your dream guy could be just a few mouse clicks away. Of course, use common sense on-line. Never meet someone in other than a public place and make sure you've told a trusted friend your plans. For some men, and women, the Internet is a Liars' Club; for others, it's a viable way to get to know someone. Wherever and whenever we meet people, we need to feel comfortable with who we are, whether our weight goes up or down. If some exotic, sixty-degree angle doesn't work in the bedroom, we need to switch to a ninety-degree position without feeling self-conscious.

If you ask a woman to tell you what she thought was her best feature, most women would probably answer, "My face." It's because we never look below our neck. To fully appreciate your body, and be completely happy with yourself, you should admire your lovely curves, and shapely figure, while you are standing naked in front of a mirror.

Mode magazine asked me to respond to the question: "Would you go topless on the beach?" I simply replied, "No." But let me elaborate on my answer. I am a size forty DD. It's just too painful walking along the beach without some kind of support. Second, and even more important, I don't let the sun touch any part of my body. If the magazine had asked me, "If you're on the beach, after sundown, with a date, would you have sex?" I'd probably answer, "If I'm on the beach with a blanket, a bottle of wine, and my husband, I might be bottomless, too. Yahoo!"

Being on *Days of Our Lives* has forced me to become even more comfortable with my nakedness. Some ease comes from my days in the theater. When you're performing onstage, you have to make quick changes between scenes without a thought as to who might be standing around. It's never an issue because the only thing on everyone's mind is the production. I am always taking my clothes off in front of Richard Bloore, the costume designer on *Days*. I just peel 'em and drop 'em. Sometimes I can't help making remarks like, "Honey, I got cotton Jockeys on today," and, "Oh, seeing the titties today, because the bra is see-through, eh?" At *Days*, I usually jump behind a curtain if someone else walks in during a fitting, but with Richard it's different—he is just doing his job. He wants to see that the clothes I'm putting on fit, and look right, for the scenes I'll be playing. Other people wouldn't look at my body in the same context. It's neither their job—nor their privilege.

As for the privacy of my own home, I'm totally comfortable walking around naked. I'll saunter to the bathroom nude, in front of Rolf, without giving it a second thought. I figure that if I let him go to sacred places, caressing and loving my body, why should I feel the need to cover anything up? If I heard the doorbell, I might throw something on, but it's not because I'm embarrassed about my body. I just don't give freebie peeks to the UPS guy.

Many of us are nervous about wearing shorts at the gym. I'm never self-conscious about how I look in workout clothes. I don't know about you, but think about it: Contrary to the body-beautiful image health clubs promote in TV commercials, I've never seen a *totally* perfect body walk into the gym. Sure, I glance at some of the men; I'll give a wink and make their day. Everyone loves a compliment.

In the privacy of your own home, don't forget compliments to your mate. He'll eat them up. Sometimes actions speak louder. If you're not comfortable with being naked, and waiting on the bed, completely exposed, for your lover, it might be better to just rip each other's clothes off. By then, neither of you is taking the time to look. Both of you are focused on one thing, and on one thing only: getting it on. Eventually, you'll get over that initial fear of nakedness and develop curiosity about the proportions, and uniqueness, of each other's bodies. It's an opportunity for intimate exploration. Everything moves a little more slowly, and you enjoy every touch a tad longer. Enjoy being naked when you have the opportunity— showering or bathing together (soapsuds can add a little camouflage); skinny-dipping in a private pool (water adds buoyancy to sagging breasts); undressing slowly in front of your lover as if you don't even know he's there (quite a turn-on for many men).

Since I enjoy being in a fascinating, constantly evolving relationship with Rolf, I insist that we keep the lights on. I've already shared the sexual intimacy, so now it's time to say, "This is the package I come in. You enjoyed the ice cream, now you have to see the carton." The fear we all have is not about taking our clothes off— we do that comfortably for ourselves all the time—it's the reaction of the other person that makes us nervous. It's not a fear of reaching out and touching someone; it's a fear of the other person's response.

Some people think love is best in the dark. Maybe sometimes, but you need the lights to help you see what's happening. You need mirrors to help you explore his body, and yours. You'll be surprised that things don't look nearly as bad as you thought they did. In fact, you might be pleased to see how nicely your bodies fit together. You'll be aware of your partner's moves and touches in a new way, because now you will see them as well as feel them.

Our fears are generally far worse than reality. If we are constantly making excuses for ourselves, or repeatedly pointing out the areas of our bodies that we dislike, people will notice our lack of confidence. If we even think to ourselves, "Oh, no, he won't like this, and I will never see him again," that man you're dating is going to get the message. Believe me, attitude speaks loudly. If you give off negative vibes about yourself, he will think, "Oh, she is really ugly," and he just might head for the door because your attitude about yourself is ugly. On the other hand, if you're positive about yourself, and feel confident about your sensuality, he'll say, "Whoa, baby, love those nipples, lay down and let me do you again!" There's absolutely no reward for torturing ourselves with a negative self-image. It's a waste of time that could be better spent lying naked in bed with a man who appreciates you, and enjoying every blessed moment of the experience.

Sometimes I get really psyched about my body. I'll tell myself that I feel fabulous. For one of my girlfriends, that means that today she's going to wear thong underwear. That doesn't work for me, but she says that, although she's the only one who knows she's wearing a thong, it makes her feel sexy to feel a little bit more of her skirt, or the soft fabric of her slacks, rubbing against her butt. It makes her feel alive, happy to be a woman. It puts a little more sass in her step, and people react to that. For me, I like full briefs in silk and lace.

Although I admire and appreciate my body, I have bad days just like everyone else. I'm sure we've all noticed, at our low-weight stages, that, where our skin now droops, our knees start to smile with little wrinkles. So what? There's nothing we can do about it. Why worry? Sure, we can visit an overpriced plastic surgeon and have it snipped, tucked, and tightened. But, personally, not only do I have a low threshold for pain, I don't see the value of going under the knife unless it's a life-or-death situation. I'm not even sure I'm ready to stop eating Häagen-Dazs; my skin might expand and, if I lose weight, start drooping again anyway.

If you asked me to identify my favorite body part, I would have to say my legs. I would rather have them showing than any other part of my body. Of course, many men adore large breasts, but I think mine are too big. Most of the women on the show work with pasties on their nipples for their own sense of modesty and to adhere to standards and practices guidelines. And they're shot from the back and side. The sheet is often down to the actress's waist, and viewers can get a side peek at her boobs. But if she has big pasties on, you can't really see anything, because those areas are mostly covered. If the wardrobe staff were to put pasties on my boobs, though, they'd be looking at the floor. While the little girls' pasties are looking north, mine are angled in a southwesterly direction. I'm so full busted that my nipples are practically underneath my boobs. So, even if I covered my nipples, I'd still look completely naked.

If you don't feel comfortable being naked, imagine how I feel performing a bedroom love scene in front of fifty people. So just relax with your lover and share intimate secrets and delights at a pace you enjoy.

8

Your Body and
Your Pleasure

How well do you know your body?

I ask because most overweight people can't even recognize when they're truly hungry. I remember watching *The Oprah Winfrey Show* when Oprah was telling her audience about trying a diet. She told them that it was the first time she had ever experienced hunger pains. Typically, we're too focused on stuffing down our feelings with food to know what our body is trying to tell us.

If we can't recognize basic hunger, imagine the havoc we create with the sexual messages our bodies try to send! We've probably spent our whole lives ignoring what we needed to be hearing. It's one reason that taking the time to know your body helps you understand the pleasure messages. For instance, how do your breasts feel when you caress them? Until we can recognize what gives us pleasure, we'll probably have a hard time understanding how our partner can do the same thing for us.

How many times have you made love and thought the experience could be intensely more pleasurable if only your lover made a slight adjustment? How about speaking up? Understanding what gives you pleasure also means taking the responsibility for asking for it. Communication is key. Being sexual with my husband is the most intimate act I'll ever experience in my life. To remain silent about what would give me pleasure is being dishonest with myself and my husband.

Some of you are probably thinking, "I can't do that. I'd be too embarrassed." Yes, you can do it. In fact, the bigger issue is getting over your embarrassment about saying anything in the first place.

From childhood, it's ingrained in females that only bad girls enjoy sex. What a myth! Women of my generation, particularly, were taught from an early age not to let a guy even touch us because it would lead to pregnancy. But once we were married, then we were lectured that it was our wifely duty to lie down and let our husbands enjoy themselves. Talk about mixed messages!

Religion is often used to repress a woman's sexuality. In several religions, we're taught that sex is to serve one purpose, that of having children. It hammers away at a woman's self-esteem. If she experiences pleasure, it's followed by guilt. If she can't control her sexual desires, then she's evil. She begins to feel betrayed by her body and resents it.

The experience we share with God is personal. The God I know is a loving one, not a vengeful one. God doesn't condemn me for enjoying pleasure from the body that was created by God. And, I also believe God is neither a male nor female presence.

Shame even makes it hard to accept positive comments from others. Most of us are not taught to accept compliments with grace.

We're taught to believe that vanity is sinful, and, therefore, shameful. The truth is that compliments can be personal gifts to uplift our spirits and build self-esteem.

Are you tired of hearing men say, "What do women want?" The next time you're asked, turn the question around and ask, "What do men want?" When you first got married, your husband wanted you to become his mother. But in front of friends, he wanted you to be the adoring wife. In the bedroom, he wanted you to come on like Trudy the Tramp—but only up to a point. If you crossed the line, you had taken things too far. The only problem is, you're never told where the line begins and ends.

Since some kind of role-playing is built into our relationships, why not exploit it? Talk openly with your husband about things you've imagined him being, or doing. Ask what fantasies he's harbored in his mind about you. Make it a game and have some fun.

Personally, I have a rule about role-playing. I don't fantasize that I'm someone else. For example, I don't role-play that I'm a size two; that would negate who I am. I might pretend that I'm from a different time period, or have a different occupation, but in every fantasy the credit reads: "Played by Patrika Darbo."

Fantasizing is healthy, especially when you share with your lover and explore different scenarios together. As for me, I catch myself fantasizing about police officers, soldiers, firemen, and airline pilots. There's something about men in uniform that sends my imagination racing.

The first thing I'm apt to notice about a man is his smile, especially if he has a warm smile. It makes me feel, instinctively, that I can talk to him, that he's an open, loving kind of guy. I also like the rugged, one day of beard growth on a guy's face. The bed head look is also really sexy. I love the natural look of a man when he just wakes up. I've never been hung up on having a lover with movie-star looks, which is one reason I don't fantasize about celebrities. I look beyond that physical stuff and into the person, trying to see if the guy is going to be there for me.

Often, role-playing offers nurturing attention to parts of our psyche that have been neglected. We may want to be the little girl who is pampered, or the princess who's captured. We can be all those kinds of things, whether we are role-playing them out loud with our husbands, or just in our minds. Though sometimes we should say out loud, "I want to be the princess," because that might motivate him to do things that he normally wouldn't. Since men are such visual creatures, we need to give them something to keep in mind.

Role-playing in sex is like starring in your own private soap opera. I think that's part of the appeal behind soaps. They are an escape, a romantic fantasy. You have the tramp, the demure woman, the virgin, the femme fatale—everything you might want to be yourself. It's role-playing every afternoon. Even better, the guys are written as the embodiment of our female fantasies. They're often heroic, will do anything for the women they love, are capable of romance, and are usually preoccupied by the object of their affection, to the point where she's all they talk about in conversation.

On *Days of Our Lives*, Nancy provides female viewers with a new opportunity for projecting their fantasies. She's probably closer in appearance than the standard size-two heroines we usually see on soaps. Viewers don't have to imagine themselves in a tiny body. They can say to themselves, "Hey, that's me!" When they see Nancy with a sexy hunk who absolutely adores her, they can also say, "Hey, that could be me!"

Any fantasy that you have, or role that you imagine yourself, or your husband, playing is grist for the mill. As long as you're both willing participants, let your imaginations run wild.

9

Growing Stages of Sensuality

You don't have that twenty-something body anymore, do you? Remember that body with no signs of wrinkles; taut skin; thick, luxurious hair; and probably fewer pounds? I'm not going to kid you, there's not much we can do about these physical changes. There are no miracle creams, or drugs, to solve all our growing problems, but there are some ways to rethink growing as a woman. As a matter of fact, I think bigger women have a better handle on getting older because our bodies and our looks have never been the only source of how we define ourselves. We were encouraged to develop other personal qualities because we were taught that our looks were of no particular value.

Sure, there are more wrinkles on the way as we age, but our sex lives will very likely explode with ecstasy once we enter our new,

mature stage of womanhood. Yes, every stage of female development has a beautiful, and positive, side to it.

Adolescent development isn't just about periods and training
bras. It's also about developing sexual desire. Pregnancy isn't only a
big belly that holds a baby. It's about a new identity and a developing
sense of sexuality. And menopause isn't just hot flashes and bitchy
moments. It's about redefining sexuality, sensuality, and womanhood.
These are not just physical evolutions, they are spiritual.

I'm going to tell you something that might be the opposite of
what you've been taught since childhood: Sex and sensuality are
natural aspects of life. Sexuality helps you develop your own definition of what it means to be female—wife, lover, mother, sister,
daughter, friend, etc. These sexual energies change at every stage of
a woman's life, but they are always there. We didn't realize it when
we were children, but our curiosity about our mother's and our
father's bodies, as well as our own growing bodies, is completely
natural. In some ways, another look at that early physical curiosity
might renew our instincts about sex and allow us to free ourselves
from our well-honed hang-ups.

Sex and sensuality play a large role in a woman's development.
They influence self-esteem, body image, weight, and relationships.
If you were taught at a young age to suppress and resent your sexual curiosity—like many of us baby boomers were—you're probably
still stuck, subconsciously, in a pattern of reacting to sexual matters
in the same way. I'm not a mother, nor have I gone through
menopause yet, but I have read and talked to all of my female
friends and family members about their sexual journeys, from
childhood to seniorhood.

Although sex has its serious concerns—like promiscuity and
sexually transmitted diseases—I want us to explore sensual pleasure
through all stages of female development. Evaluate your past, present, and future sexual development in a fun way. If there's one thing

we don't do enough when it comes to sex, it's to laugh about it. There are serious elements like emotional intimacy that I won't ignore, but now I want to talk about how changing age, size, shape, and roles profoundly affect ourselves, and our partners.

HEALTHY BABIES AND GROWING KIDS

Time and size coexist in a unique relationship that most of us are unable to understand. Now, by no means am I pinpointing one specific reason for gaining weight, or being a large woman. Heaven knows there are reasons, from ice cream to genetics and hormones to low self-esteem and pride. But another major factor is age. If some of us larger ladies look back on our childhoods, way back to infancy, we might find that a chubby baby makes for a chubby adult. It's not always the case, of course. But when it does apply, try not to use it as an excuse for why you carry extra pounds. Instead, recognize the link between who you were as a baby and who you are as a woman today.

I was born in an era when a fat baby was seen as a sign of prosperity and health. At that time, information didn't exist about lifelong eating habits being established in infancy. The fat cells that form in a baby can last for a lifetime. We're fortunate today that practical facts about babies and nutrition are as close as the nearest pharmacy. The consensus among pediatricians is that the best food for babies is breast milk. A mother's milk contains the proper balance of fatty acids, lactose, water, and amino acids for human digestion, brain development, and growth. The American Academy of Pediatrics recommends that babies be breast-fed for six to twelve months. Since I've never had a child, I have no firsthand knowledge, but my mom and girlfriends have shared their experiences and the knowledge they have picked up as new mothers.

Of course, not every mom is able to breast-feed her baby. My mom tells me that when she breast-fed me, I cried a lot. My dad decided that I was just plain hungry and fed me store-bought formula. I stopped crying, but I developed plenty of fat cells that I took into adulthood. When my sister came along, my mother found out that she didn't lactate sufficiently and fed her formula. With my brother, they went straight to the supplements. If you think you're not feeding your baby enough, or are perhaps feeding your baby too little, consult your doctor before making choices.

Today, infant formulas on the market are required by the FDA to meet very strict standards. A few moms I've talked to have thought about making their own infant formula at home but the FDA advises against it. The margin for error is too high.

I understand that solid foods are typically introduced when a baby reaches four to six months of age. Most parents still opt for processed baby foods, and if I had a baby and a busy schedule, I guess I would, too, in spite of the fact that these processed foods are often filled with unnecessary sugar.

Today, nutritional problems get worse as a child grows. Fifty years ago, we were a society of stay-at-home moms. Mothers had time, and a reasonable budget, to prepare well-balanced meals. Today, moms, whether they're single or married, typically work full-time jobs. Besides struggling to make ends meet, their time is limited. As a result, low-priced, fast-food meals are an appealing option. Unfortunately, the actual cost of fast-food meals doesn't materialize until later. Since the child isn't getting necessary nutrients, his or her schoolwork falters; the energy needed to concentrate is lacking. Meanwhile, the nutrient-starved body continues to crave food. To satisfy the hunger pains, kids fill themselves up with candy and snacks (which are advertised on their favorite after-school TV programs). There's not enough balance between snacks eaten while watching TV or playing computer games and outdoor exercise. Simply put, we have become victims of the time in which we live.

THE WONDER YEARS

The adolescent female faces unique pressures. She's struggling to form her self-identity while being bombarded with peer pressure to try smoking, drinking, drugs, or sex—or all of them. Her body also changes, seemingly overnight. It happened to me. One day I was a flat-chested schoolgirl, the next day I was ready for the centerfolds with my junior high jugs, and along with body development came sexual development and curiosity. The physical signal for most of these emotions comes with menstruation, the first physical rite of passage into womanhood. What's important for moms, other relatives, and older female friends to communicate to blossoming young women is a sense of self-respect and openness. This attitude could affect a young woman's sexual development, experiences, and communication. Positive feelings about sex and one's body don't just come from a sexual partner; relatives and society play a part. To make the first move into a new stage of female development special, positive, and meaningful for the young woman, try doing something special for her. I remember my friend's mom letting her shave her legs when she first got her period. It was a celebrated event. My sister, already wearing a bra, was twelve when a teacher showed her class a short movie about girls getting their period. She started menstruating the next day. Everyone thought it was such a big deal. I didn't. I was fourteen and hadn't yet started, so not only was I flat-chested, but I felt inadequate in another way, too.

When I did get my first period, I was on a Girl Scout campout. One of the leaders had the necessary equipment with her but told me not to say anything to the other girls because she didn't know what other mothers had told their daughters about the process. So there I was, hemorrhaging in the middle of the wilderness, with cramps, and I couldn't share the experience with my peers. When I got home after the weekend and I told my mom, she just muttered,

"Well, it's about time." She also referred to this sign of sexuality as "the curse" that would be visited upon me every month for the next four decades or so. I was devastated. I thought something great had happened, but it was met with a negative response. So, moms, when your daughter gets her first period, let her know it's a special time, to be celebrated.

You could do something nice together, like go to a cosmetics counter and help select her first set of quality makeup. At home, you can spend time teaching her how to apply it. Help make her feel confident in a very tumultuous, transitional stage of her life.

I once read a *Ladies' Home Journal* article stating that the average woman is five feet, four inches tall, weighs one hundred and forty pounds, and wears a size twelve to fourteen. The typical model is five feet, nine inches tall, weighs one hundred and ten pounds, and wears a size two or four. Sixty percent of women wear size fourteen or larger clothes. Thirty-four *billion* dollars a year is spent on weight-loss products and services. Imagine how many starving people around the world that money could actually feed.

I have friends who have tried prescription drugs to lose weight. It's worked quite well for some of them. One friend was so excited to fit into her old dresses that she dared to buy her first bikini. She exuded confidence and looked great. But when rumors flew about the possibility that one of the drugs might be taken off the market because of potentially severe damage to women's heart valves, she rushed to her doctor and arranged a last-minute supply that would last longer than her usual thirty-day prescription. She wasn't addicted to the drug. She was addicted to the way she felt. I'd rather she had chosen to live a healthier life, and maybe risk being a little bit heavier. But the responsibility for making your own decisions about the food you eat, and the lifestyle you choose, are rights that extend to other people, too. So I didn't reprimand my friend, or demand to know why she needed a dangerous pill to keep her weight in check.

We're dying not to eat. One potentially life-threatening situation that adolescent female teens face is the risk of developing an eating disorder. The media, by promoting unrealistic depictions of beauty, play a key role in making teen girls feel inadequate. Though the pressure to be thin can lead to anorexia, obesity—the other extreme—can be equally dangerous. Both have life-threatening potential, but what many young girls (and many more boys nowadays) don't realize is that anorexia can turn into bulimia, the eating-and-purging syndrome. Bulimia is about controlling what, and how, you eat. I'm sure we've all had our overeating and undereating days or stages, but the trick is to find a happy medium that doesn't make you feel guilty or controlled by what you've eaten or what you've chosen not to eat. So, obsessions with food can go both ways. Instead of being driven to overeat, anorexics avoid, at all cost, the intake of food. Both disorders represent a misconception of body size and image, and have more to do with perception than reality. It's so important for us to tell teens, right now, that they should accept themselves exactly as they are, and help them to see the personal qualities that make them beautiful.

One of the most difficult things to understand about eating disorders is that it's rarely, if ever, all about food and weight, so we need to take the time and ask tough questions of those we care about. In fact, maybe we should also ask ourselves the same questions. Be aware of denial as you attempt to be honest with yourself. You may need a second opinion, or just an objective listener. Eating disorders are about control and obsessing about that control and the lack thereof. That's why young girls need a variety of images, and role models that don't speak to one look, one size, one taste, one color, one anything! They need confidence and trust from us, their parents and mentors, in order to cope with one of the most serious plagues in young life. Annoying music, parties, and outrageous clothes can be part of the stages of development. An eating disorder doesn't have to be. Parents, watch your children closely, and pay attention to what you say to them. Be careful about how you reward appearance and size—it could have devastating consequences later in life.

While making personal appearances, I've talked to many teens and their moms. Sometimes an overweight girl can't get help because her mom has an eating disorder of her own. This seems prevalent among thirty-something moms with daughters in their midteens. It's a self-destructive cycle. Or the mother is such a perfectionist and harps about her daughter's weight so much that not losing weight is the daughter's act of rebellion. Weight is used as a weapon.

What, and how, you eat affects your body and self-image. The same is true for teens, particularly because their bodies are still growing. As we mature, life's daily distractions make it difficult to regularly monitor our size and image. A skirt that fit perfectly last week might feel tighter, or looser, next week. The changes seem to happen overnight. I cannot remember a time when I was growing up that I wasn't on a diet. Learning the facts about healthier eating maximizes your teen's growth and development.

Not long ago, a letter sent to a cable television health show was brought to the attention of producers at *Days of Our Lives*. A plus-size high school girl wrote that she wanted to lose weight to look good for her prom. The health show arranged for her to meet with a trainer and nutritionist. Ultimately, she lost fifty pounds. *Days* presented her with a beautiful prom gown, and granted her biggest wish: to attend the prom with a *Days of Our Lives* star. Kyle Lowder, who plays Brady Black, was the first actor to hear about it. He immediately volunteered—"Great, I'll go with her!"—and forever won my heart.

After all the hoopla, I asked Kyle how it went at the prom. Kyle felt bad for the teen. Once they arrived at the prom, it stopped being about her and, instead, became all about her *Days of Our Lives* date. Kyle felt it should have been her evening. Nevertheless, she was still thrilled beyond belief. But I still wonder: Did she lose the fifty pounds for herself? Or did she shed them to feel accepted, possibly even envied, by her fellow students? Her new image meant everything to her. Ironically, Kyle would still have gone to the prom with her even if she hadn't lost the fifty pounds. It goes to show that there are great guys out there who aren't hung up on physical appearance.

Both social and physical influences contribute to the confusion over self-image. Socially, teenage girls are slammed with a multitude of powerful images that spell out what it means to be sexy, attractive, and valued. Meanwhile, they are physically developing at a fast rate. Like my sister, my generation typically experienced our first period at the age of twelve. Today, it happens to many ten-year-old girls. You've probably seen these pint-size sexpots on TV, or even at the local mall. They've barely mastered fundamental reading and writing skills, yet their bodies are screaming, "I'm ready for sex!" Usually, the person receiving the message loud and clear is an older teenage boy who holds a powerful, and difficult to resist, attraction.

The afternoons that my sister's boyfriend visited, with an assortment of friends close behind, always made for interesting encounters. Somehow, we always ended up in the attic, which was also our TV room. One thing led to another, and the girls would find themselves touching the boys, and vice versa. It was always clumsy, awkward touching because none of us really knew what we were doing.

Young girls see through our uncomfortable, awkward attempts to discuss the facts about sex. They laugh about it with their girlfriends. The last person a teenage girl wants to have a discussion about sex with is her mom. They'd much rather speak in hushed tones with their female pals or older sisters. They also pore through magazines, hoping to cull new information about sex.

Reading was one way that I was introduced to the mysteries of sex. In 1956, *Peyton Place*, by Grace Metalious, was the "shocking" novel of choice. It purported to blow the lid on what was really happening in small towns all across America. Years later I was fascinated by the steamy images the book aroused in me. Now I'm sure I remember it even sexier than it was because it was the first "hot stuff" I'd ever read.

Certain pages were dog-eared from rereading as the book was passed from friend to friend and back again. It's a wonder the pages didn't catch on fire from the pent-up desire of teenage girls curious about the unspeakable wonders of lovemaking. God forbid my mom or dad walked into my bedroom and caught me reading the dog-eared pages.

Henry Miller's *Tropic of Cancer* was another book that held a fascination even if I didn't quite understand what I was reading. I only understood that certain passages prompted electric, hot sensations all over my body. I seem to recall pressing my legs together while tightening my lower abdominal muscles whenever I read that book. I didn't associate it with the awakening of sexual desire. I only knew that the feelings were wonderfully exciting and new. My, how I enjoyed spending hours dedicated to the simple pleasure of reading, alone.

I was fourteen when a worldly seventeen-year-old girl held my girlfriends and me transfixed with the private escapades she enjoyed with her sophisticated college boyfriend. She talked about how he played with her nipples with his tongue and gently massaged her all over. The way she described the tightening in her privates didn't make any sense to us younger girls, but I can tell you now, she didn't come anywhere near explaining that feeling well enough. Her tales took an unusual turn when she breathlessly recounted the thrill of licking her boyfriend's toes, and flicking her tongue against his inner thigh, which reeked with the fragrance of his natural musk. I thought I would gag! My face wound itself into a tight pinch as I gasped, in a high-pitched shriek, "Ewww!" I would take a swig of Pepsi to wash away the sordid image. Later, I marveled to my friends, "Why would anyone want to lick someone's foul-smelling, sweaty toes? I just want to know, where was her face when she was playing lollipop with his inner thigh, pressing against his underwear? I think she's a sexual pervert!" I recall the memory and chuckle at how naive we were as girls.

Meanwhile, my mom did have conversations about sex with my sister and me. Unfortunately, it felt as if she wanted to be my cool, "let it all hang out" buddy, rather than my mother. She told us about the first time she smoked. And she loved telling the stories about how the boys courted her; she often had one boy going out the back door while another was ringing the front doorbell. Mom didn't realize that we got a lot of teasing from our friends about the way she shared her teen stories with us in front of them. Besides, she was around us so often, we weren't really able to have escapades of our own. Along with that buddy approach of hers, she expected us to be more like peers with her when we had a problem. Instead of a maternal hug and some parental advice, Mom would more often tell us, "You'll get over it," or, "That's not important," as if we were adults who should be able to handle things by ourselves. Dad Don was on the road with the baseball team most of the time, so he couldn't be there for us, and he really hadn't had any experience being a parent since he hadn't had any biological children of his own.

So, instead of making me feel more open about asking questions of a sexual nature, I shut down. Though one time we turned the tables on Mom. I remember my sister and I putting my mother through hell with our troublesome questions about douching. I thought I was going to die from laughter, watching her struggle to find the words that would help her to explain why women douched. Another time, my mother remarked that she thought I would end up an unwed teenage mommy. Her reason? She didn't think I had the strength to say no to a particular young man's aggressive overtures. It made me determined to not get pregnant. She was practicing reverse psychology and didn't even realize it.

Parents today need to ask if they want other kids, or adults, teaching their daughters about sex. Personally, I wish my mom had gotten me one of those puberty-development books when I was prepubescent and already hoping to tear through a C cup. I probably would have laughed it off, said that it was ludicrous, but, privately, I would have been thankful to have a reliable resource for finding the appropriate answers to my questions. So, let me boldly make a suggestion to all of you moms with prepubescent daughters: Find a book that talks about everything—and I mean everything— and pass it on to your daughter as a gift. I suspect she'd appreciate it even if several years pass before she finally tells you so.

For anyone who's outraged that I'm talking about sex and adolescence in the same breath, let me reassure you: Sexual awakening does not equal sexual activity. Every healthy teenage girl experiences pleasurable sexual urges. It's an inevitable, natural response, not a problem. The real threat is the swaggering teenage stud who's usually a couple of years older and anxious to introduce the girl to the joys of sex. I have several friends who are parents of teenage girls. Some of them encourage abstinence, in a way that doesn't exclude pleasure and fun, as an approach to sexual temptation. They understand that it's a given that high school girls will make out with boys just as most of us did. They want their daughters to know that their fantasies and desires are normal, and that a girl is better off exploring her own body before allowing a boy the same opportunity. The more maturity and knowledge she gains, and the older she is (especially age, since I personally do not feel any fourteen-year-old should be having sex), the better prepared she'll be to make adult decisions with her developing adult body.

I had a friend in high school who thought she could get pregnant only during her period, citing her family's dog as the basis for her faulty reasoning. She noticed that shortly after her female canine was in heat, the bitch usually had a litter of puppies. Meanwhile, a thirty-five-year-old man I know said he was in his early thirties before he realized that a woman's body was designed with separate ports for urinating and enjoying sex. He learned this the day his first child was born.

I am a firm believer that all teenagers should be taught about sex and provided with the means to protect themselves against unwanted pregnancies and sexually transmitted diseases. Kids think they are invincible; they ignore the risks and make irresponsible decisions about what constitutes safe sex. Don't let them forget that knowledge is power.

Abstinence as a choice—rather than the only option—is a message teens can grasp. Boys and girls will still dance together, hold hands, cuddle, and kiss; any physical contact between a boy and a girl who are already attracted to each other, even if it's a hand briefly brushing against the other's, will stimulate sexual arousal. Some parents believe they can control abstinence by acting as chaperones who ensure that the teen couple is never, under any circumstances, alone. Give your teens more credit. If they want to be alone, they will find a way to make it happen. It's absurd to believe they can be watched every minute of every day.

I personally disagree with people who believe that sex education can be taught only in the home. Not every home is an open forum for discussions about sex, and practical sexual information will not be delivered to young people when it's eliminated from the school curriculum. In any school or neighborhood, there is always one worldly teen who's more than happy to share his or her version of the facts of life. If a teen feels uncomfortable sharing with her parents what she's hearing from her peers, misinformation can stand undisputed. But in a sex-education class, with students free to question what they're hearing, a teacher can separate fact from fiction. I believe sex education *should* take place at home, but it's not realistic to believe it will *only* be taught at home.

TWENTY-SOMETHING

By age twenty-one, young women usually take stock of their inevitable self-limitations. For instance, barring pregnancy, or plastic surgery, your boobs won't grow any larger. Nor will your height increase. The smart ones "accept what will never be," and move on. After all, the best is yet to come.

The awkward stage of adolescent sexual exploration is also a thing of the past. It's time to appreciate your body's response to sexual pleasure and develop assertiveness. Instead, what usually happens is that our emotional desire for closeness and intimacy takes precedence. Heaven forbid if you don't maximize your opportunity to secure a husband; the fear of being alone forever looms large.

Unfortunately, many of the twenty-something "dudes" you meet are "duds" as potential husband material. The young male has no interest in satisfying his emotional needs. His goal is to conquer sexually every woman he meets. You're better off acknowledging it. Otherwise, valuable years are wasted trying to achieve an unrealistic goal. If he's not ready to make a lifelong commitment, nothing you do will change his mind, especially threatening that the relationship is over. Though he may not say it, freedom is exactly what he wants. So, instead of wondering if every guy you date might be "Mr. Wonderful," use your experiences to determine what you're looking for in a lasting relationship.

During your twenties, explore who you are, and what you want. You're embarking on new careers, renting your first apartment, and establishing adult friendships. Every experience helps you to realize what works, and what doesn't. It helps to prepare you for a steady path as your thirties approach.

THIRTY-SOMETHING

Women who are thirtyish welcome a sexually exciting time. The occasional orgasm you stumbled upon in your twenties can evolve into rich multiple orgasms. Luckily, some of your twenty-some-thing duds are developing into mature men. Now that they know what satisfies them sexually, they're available to take the time to please you, but don't expect them to be mind readers. You have to be willing to communicate what it is you'd like them to do. Embrace your role as sensual guide. Take pride as their egos swell, knowing that they've brought you to multiple peaks of pleasure.

The only downside to this sexual time is that often, at this age, women feel overworked and underpaid, to the point where stress turns off any turn-ons. Without proper destressing techniques (massage, meditation, just plain relaxing), your tension will affect hormone levels, which in turn can affect sex drive and orgasmic capability. So if you can curb the causes and effects of stress, you'll be able to enjoy the changes in your hormones because you'll experience a newfound confidence, personally, professionally, and sexually.

By now you've developed an eye for distinguishing between a dud and a dude. And if you're lucky, you've found the right dude. Maybe you have married him. As a newlywed, you probably can skip a few paragraphs because you'll have no idea what I mean when I say that sex has become a weekly "appointment," or that the kitchen sink as a lovemaking spot is impossible because of the piled-up dishes and sounds more unsanitary than sexy. Newlywed sex is full of fire. You're comfortable without being bored, kinky without having to think about it, horny from something as simple as eye contact with your man. Remember those feelings, those wonderful moments, because you'll want to reach back into the memory file when household obligations, kids, job stress (his, yours, both), and the routine of life take the hot glow down to a hazy simmer. After some time of getting used to your new role as a wife, you may look back at the beginning and wish sex could be as exciting as it was then, but before you say that, take a moment to consider what you've got right now. You may not be knocking pictures off the wall anymore or getting reported for "disturbing the peace," but what you do have (hopefully) is a very intimate connection, one that goes beyond your body and into your soul. I'm not saying sex shouldn't be great, because it definitely should. I'm just pointing out that as your relationship progresses and evolves, so might the measurement of "greatness."

Let's not forget those amazing things marriage can bring to sex. First of all, you're with a partner who loves you and wants to spend eternity with you, which means he wants to have sex with you until he dies. This is good. Second, this committed relationship gives you all the time and opportunity in the world to enhance your sex life and performance with the comfort of knowing that love is the glue of your bond. And by the time you've both made vows of forever to each other, I imagine you've bridged issues of communication, both emotional and sexual, so you can say, with no fear of rejection, "Hey, buddy, move your hand to the right a little and go faster!" Marriage is your time to let loose and start loving "the one you're with" for the rest of your life.

If you thought the volume had been turned down during married sex, wait until you add darling children to the mix. Not only is the kitchen sink totally off-limits, but the bedroom experiences some changes, too. You don't want to wake the kids with grunts and moans, especially when it's likely that your headboard knocks against the same wall as that of the little ones. If that wild, unruly sex you had before marriage has dwindled into an arranged and inhibited act either because the reality of life has taken over, or possibly because after hours of carpooling and checking homework, sex is the last thing on your mind, fear not. You'll get that spontaneous passion again, but the only difference is that you might be in charge of planning that spontaneity.

Although sex might call for some readjusting and special maneuvering once the rug rats take over your house and your life, my mommy friends say that getting it on with their hubbies is more exciting than ever because there's an element of secrecy to it. This, they claim, makes for fun quickies while the kids watch cartoons, or ever-so-slow-and-quiet grinding late at night.

Also, because groping and petting is understandably taboo in front of the children, sexual tension rises to its max when both partners are prohibited from major sensual contact. Clearly, this is how quickies get started, but since time, even "quickie time," is sparse, tell your hubbie to meet you in the bedroom in one minute. Then, once the door is securely locked, give in to that tension and feel each other up before you hear a little knock at the door saying, "Mommy, I want juice." The shower is another great place to take full, wonderful advantage of each other. Let him sneak a peek at you while the kids are making their beds. And if there's time, do it anywhere in the bathroom and let the water run; it'll drown out your "oohs" and "aahs."

From what my married-with-children friends say, sex may happen less often and with less damage to bed frames and dishes, but when it does, they're reminded of how close, intimate, and in love they are. Isn't that the point?

SIZE AND PREGNANCY

Pregnancy is a beautiful step in the evolution of a woman's life. It's not something I've chosen, but many friends of mine enthusiastically agree that pregnancy and motherhood are cherished times for them.

Their bodies are busy making preparations for giving life to another human being. Pregnancy doesn't desexualize you, and it certainly doesn't mean that your days of exploring the naughtier side of your sexual personality have ended. Several friends of mine—who are mommies and plus-size—say their sexuality became richer during pregnancy. Let's start with the first, and most often asked, question: Can you have sex while pregnant? They did for as long as it felt comfortable, and that, for many women, appropriate sex can make the cervix more flexible. So get that randy girl out of the closet.

You may be one of the lucky mommies-to-be who are constantly aroused and ready to go. You might wonder why, after putting on more than twenty pounds, developing swollen ankles, and having a tired back, you are more ready for sex than ever. My pregnant pals tell me that pregnancy helps produce higher levels of estrogen, which increases libido, and that extra blood is being pump toward erogenous zones. Basically, it's a party down there. And it's not just for you. All that arousal and plumpness down below functions as a nice tight fit for your mate while increasing pleasure for both of you. You're wonderfully swollen and pumping lust throughout your entire body. Sex can be better than ever.

Perhaps you're thinking, "Sure, if I could get into a realistic position!" Size does become a factor when trying to celebrate the revived libido, but I've known several girlfriends who found a way to have fun. Think of it as an opportunity to be creative; keep it comfortable, and exciting. The most uncomfortable position is most likely the missionary position, and what used to be your hottest spot is probably your most painful one now. Try stacking several pillows beneath your hips, as high as you'd like, and have your mate kneel in front of you, and into you. Turning for adjustment, your partner holds on to that high leg as he enters you straight on. That way, the weight of your belly can rest on the bed, or on another support pillow, while you enjoy the ride.

If your legs and back get tired, or if your swollen belly is suffo-cating your lover, try maintaining the position as you slowly rotate together so you're both eventually lying on your sides. Depending on your size, you could try facing each other very closely, but if your belly is in the way, try making a ninety-degree angle with your body so that the same effect of side by side occurs. This way, your mate still has plenty of room and can reach for your clitoris and your chest. You can reach down, and around, and grab his butt, or thigh, for extra leverage.

The on-all-fours position is good, too (pregnant or not!). Add pillows under your belly so the weight of it doesn't pull on your back, or stretch even more skin. The pillows will also protect your sensitive breasts. The advantage of this position is your mate's access to your cli-toris, butt, neck, and breasts. All you have to do is balance. Just have fun and make up your own positions, then share them at Lamaze class.

My friends suggest avoiding any sex toy that involves vaginal insertion. You run the risk of infection this way, so they advise stick-ing with the external vibrator for a little shake-up. Also, don't use sex creams, lotions, or oils. They can cause major irritation and infection. All of the "don'ts" here are particularly important for pregnant women, but they are also issues to consider even if you're not expecting a baby.

Though I'm not a mother, my mommy friends have been very generous in sharing their experiences so that you can avoid sexual road hazards and detours, particularly after your bundle of joy has made his grand entrance. Granted, you are a new mommy, caring for a fragile, tiny addition to the family. One who screams, cries, poops, and pees, all at once, usually when you're trying to sleep or make love. "What's making love?" you might ask. Don't worry. It's a normal response in the weeks after you've given birth.

Usually, women wait six weeks after giving birth before having sexual intercourse. Some of my friends did it sooner, with varied results. Some were excited to be back in the saddle again, but others experienced anxiety, and discomfort, because they were not fully healed. Although I'm sure you're anxious for a world-record orgasm by now, my friends say that just lying on your stomach again, for the first time in months, as your husband kisses your neck, is the best thing in the world.

After all the new sexual pleasures you experienced while pregnant, keep in mind that after you've delivered, your husband may see you as "mommy," instead of, "whoa, mama!" His attraction, and affection, for you revolves around bringing his seed into the world. One of my girlfriends became so fed up with her hubby's reverent treatment of her that she finally screamed, "I'm a mommy, not a nun! Stop treating me like I can't, and don't want, sex!" With that verbal lashing, her husband grabbed her and allowed her sexual side to express itself again. His performance also showed that he was sorry for his misperception. You can have fun, wild sex with your mate and still be a great mom. Also remember that, in addition to being a mommy, you're probably a wife, too. Insist on time alone with your husband to reconnect as a couple rather than only as parents. Do things you used to do before the baby came. Go on dates, rent a hotel room and go crazy, buy some lingerie again and open up that dusty box of sex toys. Do this often. It reminds the new daddy that the mother of his child is also the mother of all sexual fantasies.

Life does not stop for the baby, it adapts. It will probably take weeks or months before you're comfy with your new status. Take your time and communicate with your family and friends. Learn to distinguish the difference between expected biological mood swings, which your body will need to go through in order to chemically adjust, and longer-lasting emotional side effects that may have to be treated with therapy. Seriously, trying on your new shoes and lingerie while communicating and sharing your new feelings will help you to better adjust.

FORTIES: GOOD, BAD, AND BETTER

Okay, so marriage didn't work out the way you hoped it would. Those darn dudes sometimes cycle back to duds and there's nothing we can do except get over it. The favorite advice I heard one girlfriend give another one who was recently divorced: The best way to get over one man is to get under another. Just remember to practice not only birth control but safe sex. The world is different than it was when you were a teenager. Women who have been married and find themselves newly divorced can forget to keep up with the times. Your gynecologist will not be shocked to hear you ask for birth control pills; you can buy a box of condoms without the church ladies busting you for having sex without being married.

I said that thirty meant you were a woman, and that was true, but as you approach forty, you'll realize just how much you didn't know about life, love, and womanhood. Maybe you've been through marriage and kids and find yourself alone and being pulled up that infamous "hill." Though we are taught to fear being "over the hill," let me share with you my understanding of that phrase. I don't see it as a decline in anything—personally, physically, or sexually—but rather as a "grass is greener on the other side" kind of thing. If you thought you peaked at thirty-something, wait until you're on the other side of that hill, ladies. You will know what it means to be truly sexually experimental and aggressive.

We've all heard that men go through a midlife crisis and that we're supposed to stay calm and let them work through it, right? Well, why not follow your hormones and have your own life revolution? Many of my forty-something friends have actually found younger sexual partners and have enjoyed every second of it because the sexual peaks finally match. I don't mean to say that you should go on a mad manhunt and sleep with numerous partners, I mean to say that you are woman, hear yourself roar!

On the other hand, there is a field of men on the other side of that "hill" who have spent the past forty-some years of their lives perfecting sexual performance. Ladies, don't discriminate against age. Men go through drastic hormonal changes, too, and at this point in their lives, they are said to be more sensitive and sensual in bed than they were twenty years ago. Again, I'm not promoting promiscuity, because there's nothing sadder than a forty-year-old tramp and nothing as dangerous as unsafe sex, but I wouldn't want you to think that life is over in your forties or because of divorce.

There are a few things to keep in mind, though, during this life revolution of yours: kids and commitment. If you have children, particularly ones in crucial stages of development, which I suppose is every year of their lives, then I suggest keeping the men out of your home. Seeing mom with a man who could be their big brother or new dad can be very disturbing for children. So instead of inviting him to sleep over, try afternoon romps at his place. You can break beds and dishes all you want when it's an adults-only party.

You are allowed to date and should be encouraged to meet new people, so don't let your children's opinions—or attention-grabbing manipulation—rule your social life. Back on the dating scene, you'll first experience that giddiness we all felt at sixteen when we went on our first date or had our first kiss. This will be exciting, but be careful not to misread butterflies in your stomach as love. You don't have to marry the first man you go on a date with, but you do have to have the emotional safety of your kids in mind. Before introducing the new "man of the house," make sure that your family has a chance to get to know him and accept him. A psychologist friend of mine commented that when she was a single mom and dating, she didn't even introduce the kids to her dates until they became a steady of eight months or more.

Time does not have to be the enemy when it comes to beauty, love, and sex. Instead, we should reassess our thinking and see these stages as moves toward more satisfying experiences rather than as steps away from youth. Who would want to go back to that time when climaxing shared the same odds as winning the lottery? Not me and, hopefully, not you.

THE PEAK YEARS

Have you ever listened to men reminisce about their bygone adolescence? Without fail, every guy has an embarrassing tale about an impossible-to-control erection, which popped up at the worst possible time; he was about to speak in front of his high school civics class or he stood up in a bus. The typical male teenager has sex on his mind about once every seven minutes, and the horny fellow reaches his sexual peak at age nineteen. That's right, nineteen! From then on, it's a gradual downhill slide. Thank goodness for Viagra.

Fortunately, it's a different story for women. We typically ripen sexually between the ages of thirty-five to forty. That's also the time when menopause can begin with a stage called perimenopause, which can last quite some time. It's not quite menopause, but has many of the annoying symptoms: changes in your cycle, hot flashes, and night sweats.

The media would like you to believe that menopause is a bitch. It sells magazines, other products, and gives TV talk-show hosts something to chat about, but the truth is, menopause gives us freedom. It marks the end of monthly menstruation. If that's not something to celebrate, I don't know what is. Good-bye cramps, bleeding, and buying tampons in bulk. Our emotional maturity and the wisdom that comes with that is precious. (I think we should hear music swell here: maybe "I Enjoy Being a Girl.") It's no wonder older women are attracted to younger men. We know what we want, how we want it, and are not afraid to ask. Besides, flirting is fun. Do be aware, however, that while you may be having the symptoms of menopause, you might still be fertile and could get pregnant. Don't throw away the birth control too soon.

During menopause, the important hormone, estrogen, can be depleted. The lack of this "special ingredient" is what activates wild mood swings, hot flashes, and night sweats. It can make you a raging bitch. (Which, in certain situations, can be a good thing; people will stay out of your way.) I asked my post-menopausal friends how it felt asserting their bitchier sides. They laughed. One answered, "Yes, I was a bitch, and I loved it!" But, there are medications available to ease the rough spots.

Your body determines when it's time to activate the cycle that results in menopause. Eventually, physical changes happen: the thinning of vaginal tissues and less lubrication. There are things you can do if you have discomfort during sexual intercourse. You could explain to your partner that there's no "go" until your body gives the signal. You can also supply your lover with vitamin E, or primrose oil, which are great lubricants and excellent for your skin. A surefire method for achieving natural lubrication is orgasm. Show your lover, if he doesn't already know (gasp!) how to use his hands, fingers, and tongue to bring you to clitoral climax. Or do it yourself to get the natural juices flowing.

I can't sugar-coat it. During menopause, there can be hard times, and dry spells. Some friends said they could barely stomach having sex with their mates even once a month. Others confided that they went three months before the desire to have sex returned. Take comfort in knowing that there is a light at the end of the tunnel. I have friends whose passion and sex drive eventually shot through the roof.

For some women, menopause means a loss of identity. I know women who felt useless as human beings because they had no eggs left to produce babies. Others fear losing their mates. They view menopause as a sign of aging and, therefore, becoming undesirable.

Ironically, that's why some women shut down, deciding that their most sexual days have drawn to a close. Oh fiddle-faddle! Menopause doesn't have to be dire. If your response to it has a serious, lasting effect on your self-image, or threatens to destroy your relationship, by all means, talk to a therapist. This is also a time when the sisterhood of friendship can be invaluable. Initiate discussions with your friends. Supportive, reassuring words from trusted pals can work wonders on your fears.

For those of you who are social, there are ancient, and contemporary, menopause rituals you can investigate, depending on your culture. Or you can create a ritual of your own. Also make some good, healthy food, since many of the icky symptoms associated with menopause can be altered by what you eat. Stock up on fruits and veggies. And find out about hormone replacement therapy. There are so many types, and there's probably one that's right for you. You don't have to suffer during this natural process.

And remember, menopause passes. Face the downside with strength, and then embrace the positive changes menopause brings to your life.

SENIOR DAYS

It's unfortunate that senior citizens are perceived as contributing little of value to our contemporary society. It's as if we're punishing them for what we're afraid to face in ourselves—the reality that everyone ages and, eventually, dies. Instead of respecting them for their life experience, we too often shun seniors. Here's a karmic suggestion: Treat seniors the way you'd like to be treated when you grow older. If they ramble on with tales of yesteryear, smile. Make yourself a promise about what you won't do when you're older. Of course, we may not remember that promise, so it's probably better to set an example for members of the younger generation about how to treat seniors; maybe we'll be honored for our wisdom in our later years instead of being shunted off as useless.

The most galling thing for women who are aging is the unfair double standard about age-different dating. If an old codger seduces a younger woman with his money, people either see it as amusing, and something to cheer, or they quietly gossip to one another that he's being foolish. Let an older woman get involved with a much younger man and it's a scandal. People consider this partnership to be obscene and disgusting. Regardless of which sex it is, people rarely stop to consider that the two people, despite the vast difference in their ages, might actually love each other. Besides, women reach, and can sustain, their sexual peak much later and longer than men. An older woman/younger man combination actually makes lots of sense.

As we approach our senior years, we continue to have choices. Yes, there is loss associated with aging. Our bodies no longer perform as they once did. Cherished lifelong friends and relatives pass away. For women, the chances are high that their mate will die first. By the time we're seniors, the grieving process is already a familiar one. Grieving enriches our lives. It helps to appreciate what we've lost, and to treasure what we continue to have.

People have the distorted belief that the sex drive withers away in our senior years. Nothing could be further from the truth. Like a fine wine, it mellows. Are you familiar with the song "Lovers Live Longer"? That's right; like antioxidants and not smoking, sex extends your life. So, if your aging mate says no to lovemaking, smile and respond, "Honey, you're killing me!"

Besides physical changes, our mental prowess can also diminish as we age. Depleted hormone levels can affect desire, which can have a huge affect on the intimacy and lust shared between you and your lover. For women, the ability to self-lubricate can dwindle. Just as in menopause, remember to keep a lubricant nearby. Also, as if you aren't aware, flexibility lessens. Your body simply can't perform in the same way it did forty years ago. Take your time and get comfortable. Arthritis can be a problem for couples of any age. If you, or your lover, have arthritis, be creative. For example, if your mate can't be on his knees, while you're on the edge of the bed or sofa, try pulling up a chair, or sitting on the coffee table, while pulling each other toward each other. Use the furniture, and your bodies, as leverage and support systems. Another easy suggestion, when arthritis plays a role, is to begin the lovemaking session together in the tub. The warm water eases your stiffened joints and muscles, making movement and balance easier. Since I'm a big bath and shower fan, I'm glad this works for all ages. The ability to achieve an erection, or maintain it, can be difficult for men. Besides Viagra, women can help with manual support—your massaging hand.

The senior years can be the best time for you and your lover. You've shared a lifetime of sex together. You know each other's bodies, and needs. If your senior years are spent living as a single, masturbation won't give you acne.

As you enter your senior years, build a pyramid of life experience. As you've gone through the various passages of life, nothing you've encountered is about any one thing. Image isn't just about looks. Food isn't just an energy source. Sex isn't just procreation. Everything is interrelated. Everything works together in the hope of achieving balance. As mothers, daughters, grandmothers, and female human beings, we must learn to manage our time, our love, our sex—all parts of the female stages of sensuality and identity. You are who you are, and you are loved.

10

Head to Toe

Sometimes, we let our perception of our body image get so darn caught up in our society's expectations that we don't realize that in other countries there are vastly different perspectives on beauty. While physical beauty is truly only skin deep, it's what we reveal to the world about ourselves. It's important to accent the positive and ignore the rest. Also, remember that everyone has a different perception and appreciation of what it means to be beautiful.

We tend to take for granted the freedoms we have with our bodies. We can pierce and tattoo our skin; we can dye our hair; we can wear makeup or not. Let's take a moment to be thankful for the freedoms we have concerning our bodies. At times, we may not like our bodies, and neither might the rest of the country, but the bottom line is, we have a choice as to how we present ourselves and what we choose to highlight about our appearances. It's time to celebrate every part of our anatomy.

Every fashion and fad has its cycle. Think about how fashion chooses to concentrate on certain aspects of the body. The miniskirt shows off legs, fake nails give grace to hands, tans highlight muscles and bones, hats shape faces, and so on. These fads had their cycles, disappeared, and then returned again.

You'll notice it most with hairstyles. Women in the 1920s chopped their locks for a boy-cut bob, completely shocking their hair-worshiping men. In the 1970s, there was a trend toward flowing hair, which changed in the early 1990s with a return to the short shag, and then back again to wispy, shaggy locks in 2001. The point is, beauty changes every second and every year, and that's only in our country.

HAIR

Egyptians were the most beauty-obsessed people in the world. They were so concerned about beauty and cleanliness that even workers, and others of the nonelite, were given oils and tools to keep themselves clean. Some even took their razors and tweezers to the grave with them, literally. They didn't want to be hairy messes in the afterlife. They disdained hair anywhere on their bodies, except on their heads. But even there, they shaved; even a diva like Cleopatra shaved her head so that she could fit wigs on better. So did Queen Nefertiti, who wore wigs and headdresses that accented her long neck and the shape of her face. Long, thick hair was the preference back then, and they used sheep's wool to make hefty wigs. So if you prefer changing your hair color or style with a wig these days, trust me, you're not the first woman to enjoy variety.

Women weren't the only ones concerned with cleanliness and beauty. Men used the same oils and incense that the women did.

Think about ancient Egypt. It's hot and sandy; there was no air-conditioning or plumbing. Need I say more? Shaving their body hair kept their skin cooler. Wearing tunics, wigs, and other head-pieces gave everyone the opportunity to make sun visors out of their elaborate hairdos. Also, shaving gave women smooth-skin legs and arms, another way of defining feminine identity in almost every culture at that time in history.

Hair carries the weight of status symbol and supernatural myth. Medusa had such bad-hair days with her snake-squirming locks that she turned people to stone when they looked her way. No wonder hair is thought to contain supernatural powers, and when it's cut, the powers are supposedly diminished. Other cultures believe that hair is a symbol of sexuality and freedom, and thus it should be covered up. Of course, this only applies to women. It's a matter of control for the men who force those women to tightly curl and tuck their hair up. For most cultures, the way you treat hair says something about your social status.

Though it seems like bleaching hair blond began in Hollywood, it actually originated with Roman, Greek, and Egyptian women, who loved blond wigs (the Egyptians used actual gold). Light hair, and skin, was a symbol of youth. Isn't it true that the more things change, the more they remain the same?

FACES

If you're a big girl, I'll bet you've heard this before: "Oh, you have such a pretty face!" Cindy Crawford is considered beautiful, right? But nobody ever singles out her face; they compliment the whole package because her body and proportions are the ideal, along with her face. I'm not implying that overweight women don't have pretty faces, but we also have other parts of our bodies that could be considered beautiful. When someone tells you, "You have such a pretty face," it might truly be a compliment, but in the context of how it's said, the person could also be suggesting that the rest of you isn't pretty. You can do one of two things. Simply respond, "Thank you," or study the person's face for a minute and say, "And you have such pretty earlobes." If they get confused, don't explain; let them figure it out on their own.

Using makeup is a fascinating way to enhance and transform our God-given faces. I enjoy trying different shades and colors. Of course, makeup and other cosmetics aren't just an American obsession. Women all over the world have used such products as kohl, dyes, and henna to either hide—or highlight—what's there. Since light-skinned women tend to wrinkle earlier than darker-skinned women, they've figured out techniques to cover up wrinkles, giving them the appearance of a youthful look.

As for colorful decoration used for celebrations, red was a hot color for our ancient women. In many Asian cultures, women use white powder on the entire face, and red lipstick on their lips and cheeks to exaggerate their blushing glow of excitement, whether sexual or ceremonial. In most cultures anywhere, high cheekbones are admired. American women really enjoy using blush and rouge to accent cheekbones. And it's not going out of style.

If you're hiding behind your weight, stop it right now. Try bringing out the best parts of your face with makeup. Everyone has at least one gorgeous feature. It's not going to fix an entire self-image issue, but it might open up a new, more confident you who will be ready to make positive choices in life. The truth cuts both ways: If you feel good on the inside, you look better on the outside; and if you look good, you tend to feel good. Take advantage of the makeup counter demonstration girl—without going overboard—and just have fun. You might be surprised by the results.

EYES

Eyes are one of the most revealing body parts. I love looking deep into a person's eyes and being able to guess what he or she is feeling. I love seeing a smile in someone's eyes. A lover's eyes reveal so much about emotion and intimacy that you could not speak and you'd still know exactly what he was thinking. Everything, from animals to kids, has its own sort of soulprint it leaves with its eyes.

The eye image appears in ancient Mexican culture, and elsewhere, as the eye of God, the thing that watches over you. Some people thought the moon was the eye of the universe, and that when it was almost closed—as in a crescent moon—that the universe was displeased with its people. During a total eclipse, the moon appears to be the dark pupil of a heavenly being's eye. One of the eye goddesses was, of course, Cleopatra, with her elongated eyeliner and decorated face. There is that old saying that the eyes are the windows to the soul, so many people put a lot of emphasis in making that window beautiful. Women in many Middle Eastern countries use a charcoal-like material called kohl to line their eyes. They use it to enlarge and highlight the shape of their eyes, while at the same time using it as a sort of facial glare strip against the sun. Think football lines under the eyes, but with a greater sense of beauty and precision. This has had its moments in fashion, too, for that really smoky, sexy appeal. Flappers of the 1920s knew how to use such bold eye makeup, and dark-shadowed eyes were popular for a while in the early '90s, but when I try it, I look like someone just socked me in the eyes.

The ancient Mayans had a surprising ideal for eyes: cross-eyed. They thought it was so attractive that they would hang a string with a ball on the end of it in front of an infant in the hope that he or she would end up with slightly crossed eyes. Maybe grandma was right: If you make a face like that, it might just stay that way.

Don't fret if you wear glasses. Here in the United States we have a loose stereotype that glasses are for nerds or computer geeks. (I say loose, because if a person of high status wears them, say Demi Moore, they become a new fad or style.) In Kenya, many people, men and women, wear glasses without prescription lenses for beauty's sake because they feel it helps show off their eyes. You could go from American nerd to Kenyan queen behind frames.

EARLOBES, THAT'S RIGHT, EARLOBES

Many cultures, perhaps most, adorn the earlobes with all kinds of jewelry. Some African tribes pierce them and place small disks into the holes, then periodically replace them with increasingly larger ones. They stretch their earlobes to have a hole big enough to hold a disk the size of a saucer. Personally, I think regular old earrings, in a variety of colors, shapes, and sizes, are just fine.

Earlobes are probably one of the softest, most supple parts of our bodies; most of the time, though, all they get is heavy breathing, a little nibble, and that's it. Some people go crazy for lobes whether they're long or short, full and round, or skinny. Try caressing your mate's lobes gently between thumb and forefinger. And instead of licking them silly, try soft little kisses and licks. We all have our own sort of fetish, or that place we love to touch or be touched that calms us and makes us feel close to our partners, right? Men and women often love to have their ears and lobes caressed and kissed.

NECKS

Necks have had their share of beauty press throughout history, but I'm not that conscious of the neck until someone starts kissing mine. We've all seen portraits of Victorian women who, although hiding behind layers of clothes, highlighted the length of the neck with blouses that buttoned up to right below the chin. That was either to show off a beautiful neck or to keep any skin from showing back in those conservative days. And we've all admired the long, graceful necks of Julia Roberts and Audrey Hepburn.

In some tribes in Africa, among the Mongolian, the Padaung, and elsewhere, women not only appreciate the length of their necks, they make them even longer by stacking rings on top of rings to stretch out the bones in the neck; great and greater the number of rings and the longer the neck, the greater the honor. They don't even take the rings off once they've reached a certain number. They're not for decoration, like a necklace; they end up holding the head in place since the vertebrae are so extended, and muscles are atrophied, that to remove the rings would cause physical damage, even death.

Long neck or short neck, I just say drive someone crazy by kissing, licking, and blowing on the nape of his neck. He'll get those goose bumps all up and down his body and giggle like a little boy. It's so cute. If you're after a real moan, bite gently on the neck bone just below the skull. You'll be amazed by the roaring response. Of course, every body is different, and you'll have to do your own research to find your lover's favorite erogenous zones. But it's fun to find out not only the spots that turn each of you on, but also which body parts he and you love and admire most.

BACKS

Luckily for us women, we don't have to deal with the hairy-back plague. And, although it can and should be taken care of when it comes to men, I've had some friends actually swear they think hairy backs are a turn-on. They say there's something animalistic about it, and they mean that in a good way. I've never been with a really hairy man, but I imagine I'd be thinking, "Ewww, there's an animal on me!" I think I prefer soft, pudgy, and, definitely, fur-free.

As for women's backs, we are blessed with soft, smooth skin, but we probably rarely show it, right? Showing the back can be scary since it might mean showing some love handles, but it doesn't have to be as revealing as that. The spine and the shoulder blades are such gorgeous shapes and such sensual parts that we shouldn't hide them.

In the work of the French artist Edgar Degas there is such attention paid to the woman's shape, and particularly the back. It's as if the back frames the woman's body, giving her a unique shape and grace. The shoulders, which are the main wings of our backs, also frame our personality, in a way. Think about how you stand. Do you hunch over or do you stand tall and use your back and shoulders as tools of confidence? I used to hunch, thinking no one would notice me, and it doesn't work. All it did was perpetuate the negative thoughts people already had about me because of my size. I won't let people overlook me anymore because I don't let my confidence shrink into my back and shoulders. My personality—positive, happy, confident—is seen in the way I stand. Our backs are beautiful because they support our bodies and magnify our personalities. And they are sexy, too, so if you don't have cleavage you like to show off, try clothes with a back that dips between those lovely shoulder blades.

BREASTS

A woman's chest has been the inspiration for music, poetry, and epic tales. Classical artists have always enjoyed adoring and describing a woman's chest. What's fascinating about gifted artists is that their observations never demean women, or reduce them to sexual objects. It's primarily praise and celebration.

If you've ever picked up a copy of *National Geographic* magazine, you probably know that in some African and South American indigenous cultures, women do not cover their breasts at all. There are far more European topless beaches than American; here, women are arrested for baring their breasts on the beach. Our male-dominated culture has placed a sexual value on women's breasts. In other words, because the boys can't control themselves, laws are created demanding that we cover up the parts of the body that men most desire. I'm not advocating that we shed our tops and bras and march through the streets half naked, but we should have the choice to decide for ourselves what we want to do with our own bodies.

In India, women wear a cloth, called a choli, around their breasts and upper torsos. It's like a tube top, but women of all shapes, sizes, and ages wear these youthful-looking tops and adorn them with beads and beautiful fabrics. There is nothing overtly sexual about these outfits; rather, there's a great sense of pride, value, and honor in wearing a choli. Even big-name non–Indian designers like Fendi and Armani have found inspiration from Eastern designs, with their intricate bead patterns and rich colors, in creating cholis.

In some parts of ancient Greece, breasts were celebrated and honored because of their life-giving and nurturing qualities. Greek sculptures celebrate large breasts and bellies. Personally, I think men were always a bit jealous about stuff like that, and that's why they're obsessed with breasts. Have you ever noticed how some American men squirm when they see a mother breast-feeding her baby? Take a moment to analyze *that* reaction! Breast-feeding a baby is the most natural thing in the world, yet the sight of it can make some men uncomfortable. Do they resent the attention the baby receives? Perhaps they've come to the awkward realization that something they've placed sexual value on doesn't always have to be sexualized. Or, maybe it's part of a man's "womb envy." They can say whatever they want about penis envy, but you can't tell me there's not some envy for the ability to give birth and feed a child.

I have a reason for emphasizing some men's preoccupation with women's breasts, and how we've been penalized for their reactions.

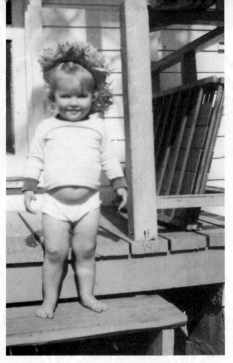

My first bare midriff top!
Fashion sense came naturally for me.

First steps? Nah, I like to think it was
the start of my tap dancing phase.

Like any good future soap character, I
got the over-the-fence news each day.

No wonder I was called Queenie.
By the time I was eleven,
I had mastered the art of striking
a majestic pose.

Rolf and I came up with this "tie the knot" photo for our wedding invitation. We had programs printed with "Act I: The Ceremony" and "Act II: The Reception."

Patrika Davidson *and* Rolf Darbo

are getting ready to
Tie the Knot

You are cordially invited to witness a
"New Wedding" Ceremony
on December 29, 1973 at 2 p.m.
at the
GOLDEN MALL PLAYHOUSE
226 E. Tujunga
Burbank, California

In the 1974 Golden Mall Playhouse production of *A Funny Thing Happened on the Way to the Forum*, I played Tintinnabula, the noisy courtesan who shook more than just those tambourines.

I used this photo for my commercial composite, which my
agent sent to casting agents. By the way, I loved the book.
When you know what to do, it doesn't matter what you wear to bed.

As Miss Fancy in the 1982 production of *Sly Fox* at the Burbank
Little Theater—I could have served dinner on my chest in this costume!

Just like Mae West said, "It's not the men in my life that count—
it's the life in my men." I had great fun in *Club Indigo Revisited*.

In the seventies, these signs were all along the Ventura Freeway in southern California. Rolf took this shot the same weekend I met some of his family. However, I didn't wear this outfit!

I'm Queen of the Champagne Ballroom, and this was the only time I was topless. Perky, huh? I did a dance number in the burlesque revue, *Bottom's Up*.

After twenty years as an actress, I was honored to receive the *Soap Opera Digest* Award for Best Newcomer of the Year (1998).

Beau Bridges and I adopted puppies from an abandoned litter when we made *Daddy's Dyin', Who's Got the Will?* Shooter is still a member of our family.

This one could follow me home, too, although it would be a long trek from Belcourt Castle in Newport, Rhode Island.

As an overprotective parent, Nancy insisted that her emotionally upset daughter, Chloe, be tested after she claimed to have been raped. In my own childhood, I often wished that I had someone so adamant and concerned in my corner. Luckily, Kevin Spirtas is as supportive of me as his character, Craig, is of Nancy.

I spent years doing telephone work that usually entailed having people thrown out of their mobile homes. But lucky Nancy has a fabulous life and a great wardrobe.

Rolf and I have a code name for kissing: SPOOOOOOON!

It correlates to the impossible standards of beauty that we neverthe-less struggle to achieve. The frustration that we allow ourselves to feel—because we can't make ourselves look like what basically amounts to a man's cartoon illusion of women—can drive us to overeat. This is what I mean when I say that we give our power away. It's time we took it back and decided for ourselves what it really means to be beautiful. Men have had the lead for too long; we should make them follow our lead.

ARMS

Arms are the spiritual tools of almost every culture. Think about it: In just about any religion, people use their arms and hands to pray. Some people lift their arms to the skies, while others clasp their hands together in prayer. If eyes are the windows to the soul, the arms are the reachers to heaven.

Arms are also sensual and physical; we use them to hug, rock our babies to sleep, hold our lovers. When we focus on the skin that sags when we lift our arms, we're not acknowledging the beauty that our arms symbolize: as a safe spot for someone who loves you. Nestled in the warmth of your loving arms, a child or a lover doesn't stop to think about how the skin sags. They simply enjoy the comfort.

HANDS AND FINGERNAILS

Recently, I watched a female mail carrier flip effortlessly through the envelopes she delivered to my door, wearing nails that were three inches long and had purple sparkles on them. In ancient China, only a member of the royal family would be allowed to treat their nails with reverence. The common woman was too busy toil-ing at her rugged, everyday chores.

How does the way you care for your nails express something about you? Hands are the emissaries of sensuality; they massage, stroke, and tickle our lovers; they provide comfort and excitement. In private moments, we can also do the same for ourselves. Treasures such as these deserve to be pampered and treated with gentle care. A little lotion goes a long way.

Whether you have short, plump fingers or long and tapered ones, with minimal care and a nice manicure, they can be very attractive. It takes little effort to learn to "talk" with them, too. A finger to your lips, a gentle stroke to the bottom lip while dreamily thinking about an answer to a question, is very sensual and often thought-provoking for whoever you're talking to. Resting your chin lightly on the back of your hand—or more accurately, *propping* your hand just under your face—can be stimulating, too, especially if your eyes continue to talk. And a little "innocent" touch of your fingers on your conversation partner's forearm makes a nice connection.

Personally, I like to have my hands caressed and massaged. And I've gotten a nice response to running my fingers lightly along the underpart of a man's wrist or palm. Nibbling and licking there is great, too.

TORSO: BELLIES AND BUTTOCKS

Just as in some of the artwork I talked about earlier, in Roman and Victorian times, bigger was better. Then, and now for some, men and women believed that a full-figured woman symbolized health and fertility. In Africa and Polynesia, for example, women dress to accent the stomach and hips. They even pad them—rather than their bras—because their men are attracted to their childbearing structure of wide hips. In Kenya, and in many other African cultures, the word "fat" is actually a compliment. For them, it also represents class. They believe that since it costs money for food, a large-size woman must be part of the elite class. Health and size are perceived as another way that the woman's body can be viewed differently.

Belly dancers have held a fascination for men and women over the centuries. These very sensual women use their curvy torsos to entice and express. In all my travels, I've yet to encounter a belly dancer with a gym-designed six-pack of abs. These women have curves and bulges all over their bodies, along with a great sense of their inner muscles and how to use them. Belly dancers are too often thought of as strippers, but the origin of belly dancing in ancient times was less sexual and more subtly sensual.

One ridiculous misconception in America is that big women can't be dancers, particularly in ballet or modern dance. It's a ridiculous presumption. In Victoria, British Columbia, there is a company called Big Dance that is composed of plus-size dancers who are every bit as graceful as their skinny counterparts. But the real beauty of their performance is in the fact that it promotes size acceptance, confidence, and self-esteem.

And if you think your behind is too big, think again. Cosmetic surgeons are getting more requests for butt implants and have developed a technique to transplant love-handle fat to the bottom for a well-rounded rump. Even the Wonder Woman doll has a fuller butt than Barbie. Fashion and favorites run their cycles, but you don't have to wait for the cycle. Enjoy your curves and know that there are plenty of adoring men who appreciate the curves . . . even when it's not the "in thing" to acknowledge this to their buddies.

LEGS, THIGHS, AND KNEES

What is it that makes men drool over legs? I suspect it has something to do with how they can wrestle with them in bed. From life experience, and conversations with female friends, I've learned that men get a kick out of wrapping their lover's legs and thighs around their bodies during sex. It must make them feel close to us, or perhaps they enjoy the sensation of relinquishing control and being locked in tight. In the sexual arena, flexibility is always key. Before you make love again, try a few leg stretches first, and then see what follows. It could help with new positions and open up a whole new world.

As for the shape and length of your legs, don't worry. There are as many men who prefer the less-sculpted look as there are those who do. I've heard men tell me they don't like sinewy, skinny legs; they want some softness that's easy to nibble and cuddle. Don't worry about your "thunder thighs." Some men equate (at least subconsciously) large, soft, pillowy thighs with motherly comfort. Moms held all of us on their laps; we lay across ample thighs as we watched TV. Love your comfy thighs!

FEET

Pretty feet are a joy to caress in bed and admire in summer sandals. Like the hands and fingers, feet can be playfully adorned with toe rings and ankle bracelets that add a touch of femininity and sensuality. Taking care of your feet the same way you do your hands offers a delicious sense of pampering and reminds you that every part of you, from head to toe, is worthy of care and attention.

Feet and toes can be a great source of pleasure when your lover is massaging and kissing them. It doesn't mean he's got a foot fetish. (And if he does, so what? As long as he travels from that starting point all the way up to the parts that you enjoy the most.)

In ancient China, men believed that small feet were a sure sign of femininity, so they would bind and tie girls' feet to restrict their growth—and their freedom. Granted, that is a bit extreme, but take a walk through any mall in America, and then visit the shoe stores and I'm sure you'll come across women today who bind their feet in tight-fitting shoes, hoping their feet will adjust to the shoe rather than the other way around. They forget that feeling good is the first step to looking good. How can you smile invitingly when your feet are killing you?

WHEN WE STEP OUT OF THE NARROW CONSTRAINTS OF our society, we discover that there are cultures that perceive beauty in ways we couldn't have imagined. Broadening my worldview after I left home (thank you, Gloria Steinem, for reminding us that we're equal in the boardroom and the bedroom; thank you, inventor of the birth control pill; thank you, '60s free-love advocates— even if we didn't all participate) has taught me to alter the concept of myself and others. The insights I've gained have helped me to build self-esteem and value myself within a deeper, more informed, context.

Whatever your size, shape, or personality, you are beautiful from head to toe, and in particular, there is some feature, curve, or texture that you enjoy best about your body. Concentrate on that and discover new places to celebrate. When someone gives you a compliment, accept it, even if you never thought your legs were the best, or your rump small enough. See your beauty and when others do, too, embrace their view.

11

Mars, Venus, Earth

Men disagree about politics, cars, and beer brands. But when it comes to beauty and women, they're of a single mind. Hugh Hefner built his Playboy empire on the male's narrow definition of the beautiful woman. Pamela Anderson is an international star because she typifies the ideal woman. It's why Hooters—a restaurant with top-heavy waitresses that prides itself on being the home of the big breasts and great buns—exists.

It takes a big man to appreciate a plus-size woman. He breaks away from the pack and asserts his own idea of what makes a woman beautiful. He appreciates the whole package; he sees the bigger picture.

Women operate on a completely different wavelength. How a man carries himself makes him attractive, not what he looks like. If anything, being too handsome can work against a guy. Unless he has the personality to back it up, he could be dismissed as vain and self-absorbed. Qualities such as confidence, a sense of humor, and kindness are factored into the bigger picture.

WHEN I PERFORMED STAND-UP COMEDY, I HAD THIS ROU-
tine about truck drivers and how they didn't want "fat chicks" and
that they slapped a bumper sticker on their fender announcing this
to the world. You've seen that bumper sticker: a silhouetted figure of
a reclining, naked, skinny woman, with big boobs and even bigger
hair. I guess it's their way of visualizing the woman they'd like to
meet. I think it's significant that this ideal image is usually slapped on
down under the truck—on the mud flaps. That must be what they
think of women in general. But it seems that *they* rarely look in a
mirror. The last time I noticed, most truckers looked potbellied and
snaggletoothed. Yet they actually believe, as if they are God's gift to
women, that a Jennifer Lopez or a Heather Locklear would be
attracted to them. These men must live in some kind of fantasyland.
Maybe it has to do with driving all those long hours alone. A good
imagination and a hot fantasy might help keep them awake. In any
case, their bumper stickers gave me fodder for my comedy act.

As for my fellow comediennes, I love Roseanne to death. When
she talks about having multiple personalities, I truly believe her,
because in a sense, every one of us has multiple personalities.
Depending on the circumstances—where we are or who we
meet—we adapt our personalities. Sometimes, to people who are
used to seeing us one way, it's as if we've become another person.

When it comes to exploring different aspects of identity, men are
so conditioned by society that they don't have the same options we
do. For instance, men are brought up believing it's wrong to cry;
they're told it's weak. The movie *Billy Elliot* was a huge success
because the idea of a boy who wants to learn ballet is novel. Frankly, I
wonder how men can truly know what they like and don't like.
There's a world of options they've never considered because it doesn't
fit into the narrow definition of what it means to be a man.

I wonder, too, if, deep down, all men are little boys who just want their mommies. Of course, they'd never admit it, because they don't want to think we're a substitute for mommy in the bedroom. Instead, we're expected to be mommy under specific circumstances and sex goddess when we're satisfying their physical needs. On the other hand, women have no problem acknowledging that "I picked someone who reminds me of my father," but we're not thinking in sexual terms. We're thinking of someone who will protect us, keep us safe, and love us unconditionally.

Women are adept at playing different roles simultaneously. The self-assured female executive uses her maternal side whether in taking care of a sick child or running a business meeting. When negotiating the price of a new car with a salesperson, we can be shrewd, flirtatious, confident, or helpless, whatever it takes to get the best deal. How far would a man get with the same car salesperson if he acted helpless and naive?

How many times has your man said, "Just tell me what you want; I'm not a mind reader!" No doubt there are some guys who are so ill-equipped at being sensitive to our needs that we wish they *were* mind readers. But, really, the last thing I'd want is Rolf reading my mind, and I wouldn't want to read his. I'm thankful that after almost thirty years together, Rolf still surprises me with some new detail about who he is. I do wish that, like many husbands, he would listen all the time instead of only part of the time. All too often we tell our husbands, often in excruciating detail, about something, only to have them say later, "You never told me that!" I don't have enough fingers and toes to add up all the times I've said, "Yes, I did. You just didn't listen." So many men only hear what they want to hear.

Yet we make a terrible mistake when we do expect men to read our minds. When you're troubled, and your mate asks, "What's wrong?", is your answer, "Nothing"? Do you get upset when he accepts that answer at face value and keeps reading the newspaper? Big mistake. If the man in your life asks how you're feeling, tell him. Don't expect him to realize suddenly that he forgot your birthday, or to figure out in one instant that you're in the mood for romance. It's about communication and building intimacy. By not answering even the simplest questions honestly, you're creating a dishonest relationship.

Also, if your boyfriend isn't particularly romantic, thoughtful, or communicative while you're dating, don't expect him to change for the better after you both say, "I do." A training manual doesn't come with the marriage license—and they wouldn't read it if it did. And if *anything*, a manual just might make matters worse. I don't think men are being dishonest while they're courting, it's just that they're on their best behavior then and forget to try as hard after tying the knot.

Women can carry hundreds of thoughts in our head: The bills have to be paid, the dry cleaning needs to be picked up, it's time to walk the dog—we're multitask performers. Meanwhile, five seconds after you've reminded your mate about something, it's already forgotten. I remember every detail of my first date with Rolf: what we ate, what we were wearing. He can't even recall the name of the restaurant.

IF YOU'RE POLITE TO A MAN, RIGHT OFF THE BAT HE'S CON-vinced you're coming on to him. But when a man is friendly toward a woman, we don't immediately assume that he's interested. If anything, we know when a guy is attracted to us before he says one word. We know how to read the signals: His body language, demeanor, and smile tell us everything we need to know.

A man has no problem ogling another woman when he's in your presence, while women are more discreet—at least in mixed company. If you know men who are very forward, and make comments such as, "Wow, look at the rack on that one," I have a suggestion. Simply turn the tables on him. When you see an attractive guy, tell your outspoken male friend, "Man, check out those tight jeans! He dresses to the right and he's hung like a horse!" Either you'll shut him up or you'll become very comfortable sharing what turns you on.

I don't edit my thoughts, and friends say that people are naturally drawn to me because I'm open. I just speak what comes to mind. Saying what you mean keeps you honest, but it can also be disarming for some people. At a Hollywood party, I noticed Henry Simmons, who plays Detective Baldwin Jones on *NYPD Blue*. I approached him and said, "Oh my God, you are the most gorgeous creature I have ever seen in my life." He was cordial and responded politely, "Thank you," but I think it caught him off guard. Later, I noticed him giving me a puzzled look. Ordinarily, most people wouldn't approach a handsome stranger and compliment him on his looks. But why the heck not? It could make his day, and men certainly do it to women all the time.

When I was a teenager, I walked up to Phil Niekro, the legendary Atlanta Braves pitcher who played at the same time my stepdad worked with that team as a publicist. Just as with Henry Simmons, I exclaimed, "You are so gorgeous!" My sister was sitting next to me and practically stuck her elbow through my rib cage because she was mortified that I had spoken to him so freely. It wasn't my intention to embarrass anyone, but Phil was bright red, too. I was just plain in love and thought he should know how I felt. His blush and shy smile only made him more attractive to me.

But you should always be ready with that quick comeback if someone says something a little obnoxious to you. People love to give free advice. A friend of mine was in church and a male parishioner came over and, without being asked, offered a diet plan he thought she should try. She was speechless. I think she could have said, "Thank you. Let's get together for coffee and you can tell me about the diet and I'll give you the details on a penis-enlargement program I've heard about."

A few years ago, I made two New Year's resolutions that have managed to stick. The first was simply to say, "Thank you," when someone complimented me. I couldn't—even mentally—add any ifs, ands, or buts. I decided that when someone pays a compliment, they don't want to hear why you disagree with their opinion even if you genuinely believe what you're saying. You might think you're being modest, but it can come off as rude, almost as if you don't appreciate the kind words. False modesty can be just as destructive as false pride.

I once guest-starred on the series *Adam 12*. I played an eccentric woman who kidnapped neighborhood cats and made their owners pay a ransom to get them back. About a decade after I worked on the episode, I ran into one of the actors who played one of the regular police officers on the show. I casually said to him, "I bet you don't remember that we once worked together." He surprised me when he answered, "Oh yes, I do. You were the crazy cat stealer. How could I forget? You were terrific!" It was a compliment that made my day. I smiled and replied, "Thank you."

The second resolution I made was to confront abusive behavior from rude people. Sometimes people assume overweight people don't deserve the same respect as everyone else. They're disdainful and dismissive in their comments. Trust me, it's all designed to make you feel bad about yourself so that they can feel better about themselves; there's only word for that kind of treatment: unacceptable. The first time it happens, I might let it pass, chalking it up to ignorance. But before the second snide comment is out of their mouths, I look them squarely in the eye and ask, "Who do you think you're talking to?" They are snapped back to reality because you have broken a pattern they've enjoyed playing for far too long, and you, meanwhile, now feel great!

OCCASIONALLY, I WILL COOK FOR US. BUT, ORDINARILY, Rolf and I are big fans of eating out. He is very hard to cook for because his tastes are difficult to meet. Rolf is also on a different time schedule. He may have lunch at three in the afternoon. If I come home and fix dinner at six, it is not going to work. If he had protein at lunch, he's not going to want protein at dinner. As far as food goes, we've accepted that we're in different time zones. It's one of the differences between us that we have to deal with.

As for sleeping schedules, I'm a night person and Rolf is an early riser. He gets up with the dog to feed him. Our dog, Cujo, has diabetes, so, first thing in the morning, Rolf also has to give the dog his shot. That evening, at six, the dog needs another shot. It's a lot of work. If I'm up first, I'll take care of the shot.

Rolf and I enjoy hosting parties in our home but, unfortunately, it's one of the few social occasions that we're not able to share. We're too immersed in our roles as hosts. But once the party is over, and long after the last guests have headed home, Rolf and I recap the highs and lows of the evening, usually as we're tidying up.

When we're apart, I call Rolf during the day. When I get home, I'll play with his butt and chase him around the house. I do those little things just to let my husband know that I miss him and that I'm thinking about him.

I'm a party person and Rolf isn't. If I want to go to a party and he doesn't, it's fine. No big deal. So, if I want to go to a loud bar, with loud country music, I drag a friend with me. I've taken my makeup lady's husband on more dates than my own husband. Rolf is totally secure with me doing this.

When I receive good news, I would like to share it with the world. But I keep it to myself until one piece of very important business is taken care of: I tell Rolf first. Anything that's ever happened to me in my career, good or bad, Rolf has always been by my side. When something good happens, the warm smile he gives me intensifies the wonderful feeling I have and makes the experience richer. I'm blessed that I can share my life with him.

12

Ah, Men!

If we've learned anything from the world of classical art, it's that the vast majority of artists depicted the perfect female form with luscious fullness and curves. And the cultural icon of a male's attractiveness was not limited to well-chiseled athletic types. Historically, men have always been able to claim credibility and sex appeal from factors other than physical appearance. I can't deny that power and wealth have always been, and still are, great aphrodisiacs. In fact, at different times throughout history, a man's weight—as a woman's and a child's were, too—was seen as a measure of wealth and abundance.

Even today, most men don't obsess about their bodies in the same way women do. I bet you have to think long and hard to remember the last time your guy asked you if his butt looked big in a pair of jeans, or if he was too fat to wear his shirt tucked in. Any lack of self-image usually stems from the size of a man's penis (or rather, lack of size, so who has the real penis envy here, folks?). In fact, some men are downright proud of their beer bellies. They actually consider it convincing evidence that they can hold their liquor. Women have a very different self-image.

The way I see it, around the beginning of the twentieth century, a handful of rich money-minded men, such as bankers, oil men, and probably lawyers, began looking around at all these well-rounded women and decided they could save money by manufacturing smaller clothes. The industrial revolution brought with it mass production, and these men realized that they could maintain an incredible profit margin if they used less fabric. About the same time, advertising was becoming a true business science. Instead of using the full-figured women that captivated the world in classical paintings, Madison Avenue hired artists to draw illustrations of twigs and beanpoles to help sell their products. A new art? Our great-grandmothers, the ones who had fought so valiantly to give women the right to vote, were constantly being bombarded by images of slender beauties in magazine ads and newspapers. They started believing that these were images of the "ideal" woman. When they discussed these issues with their husbands, the men simply nodded, like they still do today, and said, "Sure . . . whatever," and went back to talking about whatever sport was popular during that particular period in time.

Other new world developments only got bigger and better: The automobile soon replaced the horse-drawn carriage, and billboards—carrying the same "thin is in" message—began sprouting up along the roadsides. With more traveling and inventions, art museums became less popular as cultural hot spots, so women stopped seeing images of themselves as beautiful, full-figured beauties. Women became image conscious and tried to slim down to please this new breed of brainwashed men.

Fashion is constantly changing, and a man is often judged by the woman on his arm. And since men have always had trouble dressing themselves, "wearing a woman" has been their version of a fashion statement. Hundreds of years of art and culture were tossed in the trash. Even films, which were becoming the new art form, were putting slender and fragile women on the screen. Men got the idea that their purpose in life was to save us from some contrived danger, even though their own mothers and grandmothers had built a new frontier with a sickle in one hand and a Winchester in the other. On film, and in the world, fragility became a turn-on for many men. Many women thought this was just a passing fad, while others were grasping the concept. Women were given the right to vote and it looked as if they would be able to reverse this silly social trend. Women were gaining power, right? Sure, until the flappers showed up. These slender vixens with their skimpy clothes mesmerized the men, just like the sirens of ancient Greek mythology. Every testosterone-driven male in the world began emptying his pocketbook to win the hearts of these dancing fairies, and, as far as I'm concerned, that caused the Great Depression.

Eleanor Roosevelt, a large-framed woman herself, soon appeared on the scene and became a symbol of womanhood as she pulled this country together. Of course, her presidential husband, Franklin, got most of the credit because it was still a man's world and we had to be careful not to bruise their egos. With Eleanor's leadership, there was once again hope for our society, a belief that things would return to normal and larger women would once again be considered desirable.

At the same time, the world was thrust into war. Pin-up posters of Rita Hayworth, Betty Grable, Jane Russell, Ann Sothern, and others kept the boys', ah, *morale* up. Most were women of what would today be considered larger size, with ample thighs, hips, and breasts. After the boys came home, television exploded onto the scene with the incredible force of an atom bomb. Now, even the most illiterate man could sit at home, with beer in hand (he's working on his beer belly, remember?), and ogle slender women prancing through his own living room. Even if some of the earlier programs tried to offer a somewhat more realistic view of society, the commercials were becoming sexier. And one ad for Volkswagen even told them to "Think small." I know they were trying to emphasize the economical aspects of the vehicle, but the subliminal message comes in loud and clear. And let me just ask this. How safe did they think a small car would be? How roomy and enjoyable could a cramped space have been? The media was brainwashing our men— and some of us, too.

Like a reverse version of programmed Stepford wives, our significant others have been conditioned to point their sexual radar toward skinny women in order to achieve the ultimate in sexual satisfaction. The truly sensuous, full-figured women were pushed aside again. Thank heaven for women like Marilyn Monroe, Mae West, and Sophia Loren, who, with oozing sex appeal, appealed to the still sensually aware men among us.

It's also likely that after the war, women came out from behind their aprons and became more powerful in the workforce. This was threatening for some men, so dictating fashion and figure became another way of controlling women.

As I thought about all this, I wondered how the past century affected large men. As I mentioned before, they were once leaders. Their sex appeal started in ancient times when one group of burly men would fight another group with equally massive biceps in order to impress women. Maybe this was the precursor of professional football. It wasn't so much that the women were impressed by this childish behavior, but it did work out for the victorious army because women did prefer mating with men who were still breathing—and able to feed their families and provide safe homes. In Roman times, the emperors would pig out at wild orgies where women of all shapes and sizes would feed them far more than grapes. They would eat, go to the vomitory to throw up, and come back for more. And, of course, there was corpulent Henry VIII. Here was a man who actually killed his wives but still found other women to marry him. Now that's some serious sex appeal, no matter what size belt he wore. Finally, there were the large-framed business tycoons of the nineteenth century, like Andrew Carnegie, who introduced the world to the industrial age. These were big men. Round men. Men who were full of strength and power and ambition. Most of them were part of the "got-rich-quick" club, others simply cleared the forests with their brute strength. People looked up to these big men. They were the leaders of the pack. Vrooom, vroom!

The power of advertising has affected life for both men and women, and some of these same big cuddly teddy bears have developed image problems, too. Madison Avenue has turned men, as well as women, into sex objects. One commercial has two women judging passing men completely on their appearances. There are commercials for preventing hair loss, building muscle, clothes that make a man "a man."

Big men once lifted solid rock to build the pyramids, cultivated farms with nothing more than muscles and a mule, and now they doubt their desirable effect on women. They're losing their once unshakable confidence. I think this is a terrible waste of a perfectly good man. If a man has a lust for life, and doesn't keep chopped-up body parts in his refrigerator, I'll bet he could walk into any room of available women and be well appreciated. Big, beautiful, 100 percent macho material. How could anything deflate the image of these robust, sexually stimulating Titans? Men like John Goodman, Jim Belushi, Jason Alexander, and other large men are usually not cast as romantic leading men (although they still have svelte on-screen—and often real-life—wives and girlfriends) but as comedians and blue-collar characters. Why have we let Madison Avenue tell us—men and women alike—that we don't smell good enough, wear the right size, have the perfect hair, skin, eye color?

Curious, I just had to ask my buddies what happened; some of their answers shocked me. Fred used to be a popular singer and musician. He had some bad breaks along the way and fell into a deep depression. He began eating a lot to escape the pain, and eventually put on some serious weight. Somewhere between that first double fudge chocolate sundae with extra whipped cream and that succulent twenty-four-ounce steak with a loaded baked potato on the side, Fred started to associate his new weight with his lack of sex. He felt unfulfilled because he was too large. "Being heavy has a lot to do with the psychology of wondering if you are going to be able to perform," he said. And then he added: "Your partner has to work that much harder to excite you." At that point, I wanted to shake him back into reality, because size is no real disadvantage when it comes to sexual performance if you keep a positive attitude.

He also projected his problem onto women. He felt discouraged because he was no longer attracting the same women he once dated. "I have always been used to beautiful women. Beautiful women who were built great. As I grew heavier, I couldn't have that candy anymore." "Candy." I'm sorry, but these tootsies didn't sound like they were capable of very meaningful relationships. Sometimes that arm candy ain't so sweet. They're often just as shallow as the men chasing their skinny bones. I'm not saying that all slender people lack substance, because personalities, as well as sexual performance, come in all shapes and sizes, but I think I pinpointed his problem. He's stuck on a certain body type. Maybe it's a guy thing, because smart women—often women of substance who see beyond the packaging—don't seem to care that much. We will date a ninety-pound jockey one month, and a three-hundred-pound wrestler the next. Men, on the other hand, are conditioned by the media to chase a specific body type, and, now that those women don't seem to be responding like they used to, Fred's male mind shut down. He's mentally and sexually constipated because of his image hang-ups. It's not his partner who's not capable of fulfilling his sexual goals, he isn't doing anything for himself. Unfortunately, Fred's not alone in his distorted thinking.

Bill, another man who gained considerable weight over the years, seems to hold the same opinion. He told me, "You always think about the partners you have had. They may not look the same as they did, but, in your mind, you can recapture a lot." Well, apparently fantasyland is better than the real world. It's the only place where a man never gets rejected.

Thankfully, some men have outgrown this ridiculous notion. Richard, a rather well-built artist who used to be a cop, says, "Being the guy I am, my first question is about what she does. My friends wonder why I would ask that. All they want to know is, 'What does she look like?' I want to know, 'Is she smart? Does she have a sense of humor?' I like someone who can amaze me with her mind as well as her body." Richard prefers full-figured women. In fact, he finds nothing attractive about small-framed younger women.

Richard is a good example of why I often say that it takes a big man to love a big woman. He needs to be secure in himself to leave the pack of shallow men who can't grasp the concept of enjoying "more than a handful." Physically, too, it often takes a bigger man (we're talking penis here) to love a larger lady. His longer length makes it easier to stay engaged as he tips, tilts, and twirls our corpulent bodies to reach all those glorious "yee-haw!" spots.

When I asked Fred and Bill if they would ever consider dating large women, they both said, "No." Big Bill even told me, "I have seen people who love bigger women; I don't understand the allure." It never occurred to them what they could be missing. They have an opportunity to broaden their world and discover that women are full of substance and love and humor and intelligence. Pound for pound, full-figured women could be far more appealing, exciting, and adventurous than any other women they ever dated whether they are themselves trim or tremendous.

Fred and Bill are so self-conscious about their appearances that they are certain they will fail if they try. A person's batting average might slip as their weight increases, but they need to pump themselves up and approach more women—real women. "You might not get that chance," Fred insisted, "because you don't have that look across the room, that chemistry eye contact because you don't look as good anymore. But, if that woman were to talk to you, she would find out that you were even better than Mel Gibson." Duh! Can you believe these men are so dense about what they're saying? I wonder if it ever occurred to Fred that the large woman he avoided at lunch might be better than Cameron Diaz? I know *Shrek* is just a movie, but apparently Fred didn't get the point. Instead of exploring a whole new exciting world that has opened up to him, he wants to live in the past, recount his old love affairs, and wallow in self-pity. Meanwhile, there is a world of full-figured women waiting to give this man an incredible dose of good loving, as long as he knows how to love *himself.* A good lesson for all of us, men and women, of any size and shape.

That's usually where it starts. Even if we can get past the weight, sometimes insecurities stay in the way. If you take a good, hard look at the evidence, you will see that the real problem exists from the nose up. Fred let his weight control his life. Even his musical goals have suffered. He uses it as an excuse not to compete. It's easy for him to say he could've had a job on this show or that musical production if he had lost forty or fifty pounds. "You have no self-esteem unless you get to your goal," he admitted. "But you have no goal unless you create a goal." Bingo, baby. He says he wants to lose weight but he's not willing to do anything about it. If that's what you want, take a lesson from Nike commercials: "Just do it." But remember this: Losing weight does not make you happier. I have been in so many weight groups where women whine about getting back to the size they were in high school. Then they get there and they're still miserable. The weight might not be the problem; it could be the symptom of what's really eating you—anger, resentment, and hurt.

After talking to Bill about his story, I realized that he was sinking in the same boat. He was heavy as a kid, and suffered through all the abuse that the other kids dished out; trust me, I know that route. "I was ostracized," he said, "and having gone through that, it molds you for the rest of your life." Although he slimmed down and buffed up as a young adult, he hit a brick wall later in life. He said, "Just picture divorcing, a month later finding out you have a son, and then six months later, losing your job of twenty years. So I ate."

I wonder if Fred and Bill's aversion to larger ladies is another symptom of avoiding intimacy. They're stuck on their past victories—in business and in bed—and fantasy women so they don't have to risk a real relationship that might demand more of them than the one-night stands they once enjoyed.

Today, both Fred and Bill claim that they don't really eat that much. "The only thing I do is tons of Pepsi," Bill insists. We can blame our metabolism all we want, but if anyone keeps an accurate food diary, they will realize just how much they are really eating. And Bill, all that sugar! Nobody maintains a 260-pound figure on a 1,600-calorie-a-day diet. Fred tried to tell me that he stayed under 2,500 calories, but it sounds more like 4,000 when he starts talking about his breakfast, lunch, and late-night dinners.

Bill also blamed his eating habits on his parents, who now live with him. "I have gained fifteen pounds since they got here," he admitted. If you feel you have to take care of your parents, or anyone else, do it, but get on with your own life. Don't become codependent. Like most people, you probably have enough problems of your own; you don't need to save the world.

As we all know, whether we enjoy doing it or not, exercise can speed up your metabolism so that you can eat more without gaining weight, but neither Bill nor Fred seemed to get to the gym very often, if at all. "There is no motivation for me right now," Fred said, "because I am not in a relationship." So let me get this straight: He'll lose weight for someone else, but not for himself? That's not a good example of self-love. Is he seriously expecting, with that negative attitude, that one of his candy girls is going to sweep down and whip him into the slim, trim man she's looking for? Maybe he'll bump into a gorgeous young aerobics instructor on his way to the ice-cream shop. You can't sit around waiting for the right person to show up and make you happy. You have to be happy in order to attract that person. Two miserable people coming together, trying to make each other happy, is like two negatives added together: still a negative. Everybody brings their own baggage to the relationship, and when those bags are opened behind closed doors, watch out. It can make Hurricane Andrew look like a summer drizzle.

If these guys would wake up with a positive outlook, they would be amazed by how far they could travel on their energy alone. Look at me, I'm happier than ever and busy as a bee! Sometimes it's hard to push ourselves because we have so many issues to confront, but that's why there are support groups where people can interact with other people who have the same problems. If Fred and Bill truly want to meet someone special, maybe they should go to Weight Watchers instead of hibernating at home.

Some people just have a fear of intimacy. From listening to these guys, and realizing how much they miss the past, I sense that something substantial is lacking in their lives. "I love sex, I love it," Fred told me, "and I would have it every day if I could, preferably with fifty different women. But until I lose this weight, I won't feel good about myself, and that is the bottom line." How sad. If he would focus on finding one person to love him, rather than fifty women to screw, he'd be able to experience a passion that he has never felt before.

Although math isn't my best subject, I've reduced my thoughts into one easily digestible theory: Weight plus manipulative advertising multiplied by emotional baggage and mental outlook equals a negative self-image. Not bad, eh? However, since every reaction has an opposite and equal reaction, a positive self-image can be achieved by the following equation: Poor self-image minus guilt and denial divided by your own positive reinforcement equals eternal happiness. Who needs Einstein?

These men need to get their butts out there and start mingling. Ms. Right is not going to pop out of their closets as they sit at home munching Ding Dongs. Of course, maybe they have blow-up dolls stashed in their closets but, if that's the case, that's something I can't even begin to address.

And finally, in case you haven't already guessed, my point is not to pick on men—big or otherwise. Many of the issues Fred and Bill are dealing with are the very same ones we women prefer not to address. We can use our weight, our negative self-image, not to participate in life and love. Don't let the media or anyone else tell you there's something wrong with how you look. Get over it and celebrate all that makes you the wonderful, beautiful woman you know you are!

13

Sex, Food, and All Kinds of Emotions

I started using food to comfort myself when my parents were going through their divorce. Occasionally, I look back at childhood photos of myself growing up and see a happy, smiling—and slim—child before my parents divorced and we were living with my grandmother. I felt safe, cared for and loved. Later, when my siblings and I were shuffled from Grandmother's house to our stepparents' homes and our mother was on mood-altering prescription medication, I was at the mercy of her mercurial reactions. Food became the only thing I could control; I chose what and when to eat. Food became a comfort and a drug to stuff down emotions—hurt, anger, disappointment, sadness, feeling abandoned—that I didn't understand and was not able to handle.

Parents who have overweight children try a variety of methods to control the kids' appetites. They badger the child, place restrictions on eating between meals, or try to shame them about overeating. Some overreactive parents even take the kid to a diet doctor and try to obtain prescriptions for appetite suppressants. My mother, grandmother, and stepmother tried all of that with me. As with most overweight kids, nobody bothered to take me to a psychiatrist to figure out what the hell was really wrong.

I was never allowed to express anger as a child. If I raised my voice, even in defending myself against an untrue accusation, I'd get smacked. If I pointed out that Mom's reaction was unfair, I'd get whacked harder. I was told, "You have no right to be angry. If you don't like it here, leave!" Where was a preteen kid to go? I went to my room and ate. It wasn't a perfect childhood, but most of us never had that, and my sister, brother, and I turned out all right. The adult part of me knows our mother did the best that she could under the circumstances. The child part of me still hurts.

Now I cry all the time. It's my only emotional release because I'm still unable to yell or scream. A few years ago, I enrolled in a self-defense class. I couldn't say "No!" in a commanding way. Instead, when a person came at me to attack, I cried. I became the five-year-old kid who couldn't say no to defend herself.

I constantly worry about the things I can't control, even when it doesn't directly involve me; I get angry about them. I'm sometimes unable to read a newspaper or watch the news on TV because the reports are often so upsetting. There is so much that needs to be fixed in the world. I know I can't do it, but at the same time, it bothers me. I wonder what it is in other people that makes it possible to not be affected by the things that I obsess about. My own husband, who is a true humanist, tells himself, "If I can't control something, or change it, I'm not going to invest energy in worrying about it." It has created very emotional arguments between us.

Once, we were driving on a crowded road with speeding traffic. I spotted a stray dog in one of the lanes and wanted to stop and rescue it.

But Rolf kept driving. He understood what I couldn't. By leaping into traffic to rescue the dog, there was the danger I would be struck by an oncoming car. We went the entire drive without speaking. It wasn't until days later that I realized Rolf was looking out for me in a way that I wasn't prepared to do myself. (Yet I still haven't forgiven him.)

I THINK THERE'S ALMOST ALWAYS AN EMOTIONAL TRIGGER before a weight gain. Eating might seem like a physical act, but it's emotions—whether we're aware of them or suppress them—that drive us to overeat. Though I often wear my emotions on my sleeve, I try to hide them with a happy smile. Then I get home and let it fester until it becomes an infected, emotional abscess. I'll sit and stew, thinking, "What did I do to deserve this?" Fortunately, I've also learned to ask, "How can I help my feelings to move on?" One way that helps is to sit down and write out my feelings, free form, without censoring my thoughts. It provides me with an opportunity to see the bigger picture and snaps me out of the obsession. Once you release the pain, you can begin the process of healing.

One way to take your mind off eating is to find a hobby. I enjoy taking voice lessons because when I'm home practicing, my concentration is so focused that I don't think about anything else. I've also enrolled in dance classes: tap and jazz, and swing with Rolf. The next class will be Latin salsa. If you're afraid that you'll be embarrassed because you don't feel graceful or because you're the oldest one there, stop making excuses. There are many classes for adults, from beginners to advanced. Men and women way over thirty are in my jazz and tap classes. Many there have performed on Broadway in the original production of *Company*. I've tripped the light fantastic with Alan Seuss from *Laugh-In*, producer Billy Barnes, and several original Mousketeers in class, too. We stretch and dance for about an hour and a half twice a week and have a great time. Join a class. You might find, like I did, that you're the youngest in the group. It feels good to be seen as the "kid" again. Besides learning fun dance routines, I am also receiving the benefits of exercise.

Sewing is a hobby that completely relaxes me (except when I get pricked with the needle). Besides sewing for myself (I made my own wedding dress!), I sewed costumes for a community theater company while Rolf built sets. We'd work our regular day jobs and then work all evening at the theater. We had a great time. I always loved the period productions. I made the baseball uniforms for *Damn Yankees*, and for another play, *Leave It to Jane*, which was set in the 1890s. I put together reversible skirts and blouses. There were other plays, including *A Funny Thing Happened on the Way to the Forum, Ladies in Retirement, Wish You Were Here*, and *Bye Bye Birdie*. It was a lot of work, but the fun was beyond measure. It's a good feeling to get out and share your talents. Most people don't realize that when you're sewing for the stage, it doesn't have to be perfect. The audience is rarely seated close enough to notice.

Some people meditate. I've tried it, but I still have too many blocks. When it becomes too quiet in my head, I feel alone, which frightens me; perhaps it's some deep-rooted fear of abandonment. To distract my thoughts, I've actually walked through the house, from room to room, and have automatically turned on every television. The noise makes me feel less alone.

I've used food as a tranquilizer, almost like some people use drugs, in order to escape problems and emotions, but I am fully aware of what I'm doing when it comes to food. One reason that I exercise is because I know my drug of choice is Häagen-Dazs ice cream. I usually reach for it when I'm feeling low. (Thankfully, Kristian Alfonso, who plays Hope Brady on *Days of Our Lives*, introduced me to Carbolite ice cream. It has no fat, no sugar, and only nine grams of carbohydrates per six ounces. I'm eternally grateful to her!)

Sometimes when I'm feeling blue, I eat over it, and that creates a vicious cycle. There was a time when I would eat a bag of Oreo cookies, only to experience feelings of shame and remorse. To avoid the feeling, I'd just head for the kitchen and find another snack. Now, before I reach for the Oreos or any other high-calorie, sugar-laden, high-fat food, I try to make it clear to myself *why* I'm eating. I also visualize the feelings I will probably experience when I've finished snacking. Granted, I might still be eating a bag of cookies, but I'm not suffering from the aftermath of the guilt, the feeling that sent me reaching for a second bag. I think of it as a proactive approach.

Weight-loss diets, and everything related to them—the special food programs, exercise gurus, over-the-counter pills, prescription drugs, books, and magazines—are a multibillion-dollar business. Some of us will try anything, even risk dangerous side effects, to look good. If a miracle pill was developed, the weight-loss business would go belly up. Think of it this way: They get financially fat convincing us to believe they have the quick fix to make us thin. Of course, I still fantasize about that miracle diet product. If there was a weight fairy who granted wishes for a perfect body, I'd be pushing and shoving everyone out of my way to get to her.

We can't pick up a magazine these days without reading about someone else's weight loss. If we follow their plan, we, too, can shed pounds. Every week there is another woman on the front cover of practically every magazine who promises to tell you how to lose weight. Oprah Winfrey's magazine, *O*, is a breath of fresh air and a wonderful alternative to all the bunk about crazy fad diets. *O* doesn't promote negative self-images about being heavy. The atti-tude is, "If you are heavy, and you feel miserable, find out what's really making you feel bad about yourself. If you want to lose the weight, then lose it."

I have friends who have tried all kinds of diets: high-protein, low-sugar, low-carb, you-name-it diet. Every single one of them complained about how badly they missed sugar. Personally, I've found that I can go several months without sugar and feel just fine. But I cannot have even just half a dessert without triggering a sugar binge. Taking the first bite of sugar is like an alcoholic taking the first drink of a binge, or a recovering drug addict taking a first hit after cleaning out.

For those of us who are plus-size, we need to be diligent in not making food our primary relationship, but that doesn't mean you have to deprive yourself. What I've learned during my journeys through diets, bingeing, and starvation is that I *like* food. I don't want to have a screwed-up relationship with it. I want to enjoy a piece of chocolate cake but I'll have some Carbolite ice cream instead and not suffer any guilt. I'd also like to snack on veggies and fruit without feeling as if I'm punishing, or depriving, myself. How do I do that? I try to balance my diet with the things I love, and the things I know will help my body function and feel good internally and externally. It's taken a lot of experimentation and diet fads to get me here, but I know what makes me happy and what doesn't.

I've learned to balance my food to balance my soul. You won't feel guilty about having that warm doughnut once in a while if you know that it won't destroy your sense of peaceful balance. Enjoy food by learning about how it makes you feel.

I know that after I split a loaf of French bread, and dipped it into a rich dip or sauce, with my husband or dinner guest, I felt heavy, tired, bloated, and just plain blah. I haven't removed carbohydrates like bread and pasta from my diet, but I'm training myself to develop balance. I eat more protein than carbo-rich foods. Carbohydrates get transformed into glucose (sugar), which then turns to fat. Try adding more protein-rich foods and eating less carbs and sugars and I guarantee that you'll feel different.

Many fad diets advocate living like cavemen and cavewomen by eating nothing but berries and meat or limiting a diet to sprouts and seeds. Who wants to do that? Not me. I've taken the best parts of all the diets I've tried—especially Weight Watchers' low-fat and no-skipped-meals approach and, for a short period, the Atkins high-protein—figured out how they fit in with my personality, and found a solution that pleases me. That means no sugar, plenty of vegetables and fruits, and some protein. It might take some time to decide what fits you best, but take that time. It's worth a healthy friendship with food! I try (it doesn't always work and that's fine) to avoid a lot of sugar.

The hardest part about eating healthily is that it's not usually convenient. Think about it. What's in your pantry? Probably crackers, cereal, rice, instant batter, cookies, pasta, and sauces. All carbohydrates. So instead of saying, "Gee, I would eat a fruit salad if only I had the fruit cut up already," I set aside time to slice big batches of fruit, which I keep fresh in a Tupperware bowl inside the fridge. That way, when I get the munchies, watermelon, strawberries, honeydew, oranges, kiwis, and grapes are all waiting conveniently for me.

I won't lie, I'm not an exercise freak. I don't like it that much at all, but I do make an effort here and there to move my body. You don't have to be a power stepper, or on the basketball or track team to move your body. I'll make a day when I sprint up my stairs every time. It's no kick-boxing class, but I get a great burst and the pain is short-lived.

Primarily, I've addressed big and beautiful women. But there are women on the opposite end of the spectrum who can't gain a pound, no matter what they eat. Usually, they have figures that resemble that of a preadolescent boy. Though they're not overweight, the struggles they face, such as a desire to attain the perfect body, and being preoccupied with food, are similar to what we face. But it manifests itself in a different way; instead of trying to starve themselves with trendy diets, they're usually busy trying to gain weight with extra milk shakes, peanut butter and jelly sandwiches, and meals that are smothered in rich, creamy sauces.

Ideally, no one should have to beat themselves up about size, overweight or skinny. Often, it's easy for us overweight gals to resent our slimmer sisters. They didn't create the mind-set that values their appearance over our rounder version. If you're heavy, try to remember that everyone has challenges to overcome. Just because their appearance is thin doesn't mean there aren't eating issues that need to be confronted. You might be surprised to know that there are a lot of rail-thin starlets in Hollywood who attend Overeaters Anonymous. If your food controls your life, it doesn't matter what size you are. The important thing is to deal with it.

My manager, Bobbie Edrick, who is always dieting is one of those people who can actually say, "Oh, I've been so busy that I forgot to eat." The concept is alien to me. How could you possibly forget to eat? You can forget where you put your keys, whether you paid last month's utility bill, or what time you're supposed to pick up the kids. But how can you possibly forget to eat? It's like forgetting to breathe! That's a memory lapse I'd love to experience.

Looking at the cover of any fashion or celebrity magazine, it's easy to believe that beautiful people are revered by everyone. As hard as it might seem to accept, beautiful people have their problems, too. Think of it this way: When a person is blessed with financial wealth, he constantly has to wonder, "Why does this person want to be my friend? Does he really like me for me?" The same process applies to a beautiful woman. Often, the people they wish would approach them at a party stay away because of insecurity. "She's too beautiful and glamorous to have anything to do with me," the other party guests whisper. Meanwhile, the beautiful woman's shyness is mistaken for deliberate aloofness, as if she's better than anyone else. Finally, the beautiful woman is cornered by the exact people she'd prefer to avoid, people who place value on something that has nothing to do with the person inside. So, as someone who stars on a show with dozens of gorgeous stars, I think beautiful people have it just as tough, but in a different way. When they're in a room full of strangers, they'd welcome the attention from an open, warm, friendly person.

When I commit to a healthier food plan, I rarely discuss it. Past experience has taught me that I'd rather not deal with those well-meaning friends, also known as "the food police." You know the type; once they know you're trying to eat healthier, they make it their personal mission to keep you on it. If you're walking through a mall, and there's a Mrs. Fields up ahead, they immediately veer you in the opposite direction. You see, they know better than you that the mere scent of a chocolate chip cookie baking will shatter your fragile willpower. Instead, they'd rather introduce you to a sensible new treat available at the healthy juice bar—wheat grass. You know the slimy clumps of grass that get trapped in the blades of your lawn mower cutter? Now imagine running that through your juicer and then drinking it. Calling Mrs. Fields! One chocolate chip cookie, please, to keep me from gagging!

Heaven forbid that you're stuck with a member of the passive-aggressive food police squad. She won't say what you shouldn't eat. That's too direct. Instead, she marches you through the food court at the mall, and when she catches you lingering to gaze at the McDonald's menu, she reprimands you with a recriminating look. However, it is a successful form of aversion therapy. I simply avert spending time with her.

Allowing people to treat us with such rudeness is another way in which we give up our power. We know it's unacceptable, but we rarely stand up for ourselves. Instead, we listen to the deceptive part of our mind that says we deserve the treatment because, after all, we are overweight.

I remember participating in a fund-raising walk for a kids' charity. It was early in the morning; I had my hat and T-shirt on, ready to begin the walk. In the area near the starting gate, a guy set up a small table where he attempted to sell people energy bars for the walk. I was with a friend who he hailed over for a sample. It looked like two tiny pieces of bread that didn't quite rise enough. It had plenty of fiber, but the pieces were also dusted with cinnamon and sugar.

I turned one of the packages sideways to read the label. It had less protein than a Cheese-It cracker, and more carbohydrates and sugars than a powdered doughnut. I said, "This is a lot of carbs. Not for me, thanks." He gave me a dismissive look and asked, "Do you exercise?" I told him, "Yes, I exercise. Would you like to meet my trainer/nutritionist so she can help you with product improvement?" Even at a walkathon, there's always the one guy who thinks it's okay to beat up on "the fat girl."

We're far too concerned about what other people think, and we allow them to influence how we think about ourselves. If we could develop a strong sense of self, and believe that beauty truly is in the eye of the beholder, we'd win half the battle. I also know that how we see ourselves influences the way other people see us.

We also need to get past trying to figure out why some men prefer skinny models. It's subjective. It's also probable that men have been corrupted by the media, just as we have. They're so used to the media telling them what they're supposed to think of as beauty that they don't give it a second thought. If there's any responsibility we can take in changing their perception, it's by offering alternatives to open their minds. Media is about manipulation. Did you know that photos of female celebrities and models that grace the pages of many popular magazines are often computer-altered? Rib cages and hips are narrowed to make the woman appear thinner. On a subliminal level, it reinforces an impossible-to-reach standard. If we don't become comfortable with ourselves, we usually go too far in one direction or another to try and make ourselves fit the standard. It shouldn't be about whether you are big or small. Find ways to show your husband that bigger can be better.

There are so many other things that are important in life. It goes by so fast. What a waste it would be to spend our lives wishing we could be perfect, wishing we had lost twenty more pounds. I know far too many women who stop living while trying to lose the weight they think is holding them back. They refuse to leave the house. I've yet to meet a couch potato who lost weight sitting in front of the television. Get out of the house. Visit friends. Go to that party anyway. Walk around the block. In the process of living, you might actually lose the weight you thought was holding you back.

Here's another feel-good-about-yourself suggestion: Go to the opera or watch it on your PBS TV network. Sit and enjoy the big, beautiful women performing onstage. Did you know that one reason opera singers are big is because they need the weight to sustain certain notes? Opera singer Margaret Jane Ray explained to a television interviewer that a large lung capacity creates power from within. You'll notice that the male singers are usually big, too. Frankly, I love everything about the opera: the singing, the splendid sets, the period costumes, and the huge orchestra.

There is nothing I could do thin that I can't do now. One thing that I hear big women lament is, "If I were thin, I would wear a bikini and bask in the sun." Consider yourself fortunate that you're not sitting in the sun baking your skin to a fine crisp. Besides the possibility of skin cancer, the sun's powerful rays age your appearance faster than anything. Admit it. If you've been a hefty gal all your life, don't you get a secret sense of enjoyment when you see how much older your skinny peers from high school now look? While we spent our teen years sitting cool in the shade, our bikini-wearing classmates did damage to their bodies that didn't show up for decades. But there's an even smarter reason for staying out of the sun. Melanoma is the number one cancer right now. It's also the easiest form of cancer to prevent. Simply avoiding the sun's harsh rays significantly lowers your chances of developing skin cancer.

Though I refuse to tan, I do like to have a good skin tone. I've noticed that being heavier, my body does look better with color on it. I use self-tanning lotions to add skin tone. Stretch marks, or other imperfections, disappear or are at least camouflaged, and the contours of my skin look different. So I understand why people would want to tan; I simply use a different approach. There are several good tanners on the market that don't leave streaks or turn your skin the color of a carrot. When I use a tanning product, I start at my toes and work all the way up, including under my arms, to the base of my neck, about to the collarbone. I don't apply lotion above the neck. Our face color is always changing, depending on makeup and unavoidable daily exposure to the sun. Rolf helps me with my back and all the parts I can't easily reach myself.

Tan or pale, whenever I've lost weight, I've noticed that some women friends treat me differently, as if I have betrayed them, or somehow have let them down. Getting the cold shoulder from our overweight pals does more damage than we realize. These are the women who have usually been our companions and support system when we didn't believe anyone else was interested. It's sad to think that, by losing weight, we lose their friendship. There have been times in my past when I broke my diet because I couldn't cope with the fear of being friendless. But I haven't always realized that whether I'm a size eight or an eighteen, there are people who love me anyway. Folks, it's yet another area where developing confidence, and building self-awareness, is extremely important. The only fear we really have to tackle is the one we imagined.

IN HIGH SCHOOL, I WENT ON VERY FEW DATES—NOBODY wanted to be seen taking out the "fat girl." In college, I joined the theater group, where I got plenty of male attention—from the gay drama students. Don't get me wrong; I love the gay pals I made in high school. Some of the gay male friends I made in college were pretty cute—and affectionate. But if we're not careful, we can use our gay buddies to feel even worse about ourselves. It would have been very easy for me to slip into thinking, "If I could get them to see the real me, and love me for who I am, maybe they would go straight." Uh-huh. And maybe one day Elton John will even write a love song about me. Accept people as they are, not as you might want them to be to fulfill your own fantasy.

Before I moved to Los Angeles, I lived in Atlanta, where I studied theater. After acting classes, a group of us would relax at the local bar. I felt happy and carefree because I was studying what I enjoyed and living in an exciting new environment. I weighed about two hundred and twenty pounds. One night, three or four of my girlfriends were already at the bar, talking with a couple of guys, when I entered with another girlfriend. Seated on a stool next to me was a guy I didn't know, and we got to talking. He told me about a motorcycle accident that he had survived. He had been at the bar for a while and my insecurities told me that the only reason the guy bothered talking to me was because he was drinking; his speech had a slight, but perceptible, slur. While we talked, he took my hand in his; it was a very sensual gesture. As the conversation progressed, I became aware that the other parts of my body were reacting to this touch. When we got up to say good night, I realized that the reason he slurred his words was because of injuries from the motorcycle accident. He also had a limp, and one of his hands was lame. I was flushed with embarrassment and hurried to leave the bar. While we were seated, everything was fine. But once I became aware of his physical shortcomings, my reaction toward him completely changed. I'm embarrassed to say that *I* was worried about what my friends would think of *me* for being with *him*. Rather than appreciate his good qualities, I became focused on the things about him that might cause people to judge me: "The handicapped guy is all the fat girl can get." I was young and stupid and the memory of that night still makes me feel bad. That experience stayed with me long after I forgot other details of my life in Atlanta. I came to realize that I could take my shame and use it as an opportunity to remind myself that I, too, have judged people solely on the package presented. It helped me to see that there are others, besides overweight people, who suffer prejudice. If I could find that man today, I would embrace him and tell him how sorry I am for acting so horribly all those years ago.

When I moved to California in the early seventies, free love, among other things, hovered in the air. I didn't have boyfriends because I didn't indulge in that attitude myself, but I did gain some insight through the experience of several girlfriends. They'd meet a guy they were attracted to and have a three-day fling—usually, encounters that were fueled by alcohol and curiosity. When they didn't hear from the guy again, they'd blame themselves. Remember, we had all come from a generation that was taught to believe, "If a girl leads a guy on, she deserves what she gets."

Those of us with low self-esteem find that our people-pleasing tendencies can make us easy prey in the sexual arena of dating. We long for the affection and physical contact, and a sexual encounter is a reasonable facsimile, but especially when it's followed by neglect, we blame ourselves. There *is* such a thing as being sex-starved (more accurately, love-starved), and in that state, you're not going to make the wisest choices.

Also, dating can be tough for plus-size women who are trying to watch their figures, since much of dating revolves around food. Think about it. You're at a baseball game and tempted by mouthwatering hot dogs. You go bowling, roller skating, or ice skating, there's always a nearby concession stand offering ice cream or hot chocolate. How about a movie? Who can resist the warm, heavenly scent of popcorn as you enter the lobby?

I have found a way to deal with the relationship between food and dating. I always enjoyed first dates in a quiet restaurant, where we could have a nice meal and talk without anyone bothering us. Eating a good meal helps me to relax; I feel less guarded, less inhibited. If things weren't going well, I'd order dessert. If everything was fine, and the chemistry was there, I'd still get dessert. Think of it as "having your cake and eating it, too." If you're feeling happy, and you'd like dessert, let it be part of the experience. Why deny yourself when you're feeling good? Remember, everything—including food and sex—is best in sensible moderation. Often, the denial is what leads us to overeating. Let's say your date has kissed you good night at the doorstep and then left, clearly never intending to call you again. You walk into your house, and though your mind is on him, it's also preoccupied with that dessert you passed on. You head for the kitchen and overindulge in a family-size bag of Oreo cookies.

You have far less control over other people's attitudes and behavior than you do over your own, but you can speak up for yourself. I have a playwright friend who has always been extremely body conscious. He was a fat kid who was tormented by his brother and the neighborhood kids. As an adult, he's had liposuction and spends several hours daily on his exercise bicycle. In my presence, he comments on other people's weight. Often, I've said, "Are you forgetting who you're talking to?" His response: "I never think of you as overweight." I chose not to dump this particular pal because he has several redeeming qualities, and is essentially a good person. I do call him on his behavior. Otherwise, I'd probably hold so much resentment that I'd go home and eat because of it.

Be aware of your emotions and stand up for yourself when it's appropriate to do so. It's empowering not to let people or food control you.

14

Lusty Ladies

Women of the Amazon have always held a world of mystery for me. Though they were fierce killers who waged a brutal war against their male counterparts, they projected an image of supreme strength and majestic beauty. Some of the soldiers they captured were sentenced to perform back-breaking chores. When they grew exhausted, their limp, lifeless bodies were tossed in the trash heap. The Amazons held Olympian gods in higher esteem, making time to engage in passionate affairs with those mighty figures. Amazon women, particularly, worshiped Artemis, goddess of the hunt, and looked upon Zeus as their personal "stud muffin."

Speaking as a woman who's nearing the midway point of life, I'd like to share the life-affirming lessons that the amazing Amazon women have taught me. It is in sharp contrast to the self-serving misinformation perpetuated by insecure male historians. My perspective of the women who once ruled the world will, particularly, inspire those of you who carry the personal awareness that your once elastic flesh is growing weary from its daily battle with gravity.

The mighty Amazon warriors knew the secrets of womanhood. What we now consider as negatives, they viewed as positives: Drooping breasts were a status symbol, cellulite was a sign of fertility, and a big butt was an aphrodisiac, luring enchanted men into their web of passion. They didn't lie passively as their male lovers climaxed and then withdrew. Instead, they patiently trained their lovers in how to find the G-spot.

Greek historians tell us stories about vicious women who would not permit their daughters to marry until after they had slain an enemy in battle. The enemy, of course, was male. As these tales have been passed down through the ages, people have listened in horror, their minds conjuring up visions of such blood thirstiness.

But stop to consider the bigger picture and it all fits. Amazon women simply eliminated a bunch of potential jerks, but spared the cute ones so they could repopulate the world. Anthropologists have discovered graves of Eurasian nomads and uncovered remains of men holding clay cooking pots and the skulls of small children. These women knew how to train their men. It sounds like a system that needs to be reintroduced.

Picture this: The Amazon woman lures her man into her bed. The prospective mate—tall and muscular, long flowing hair cascading down his back (think Fabio)—is hypnotized, fascinated by her jiggly butt and swaying breasts. As she wraps her puckered thighs tightly around his waist with a passionate power, he understands that his role is to provide at least one magnificent orgasm (but the more the better), or risk being made into tiger bait. He is a man who lives solely for her pleasure.

When the gods of Olympus were not fighting over Amazon women, the gods battled their bitter foes the Titans. The seeds of one particularly noteworthy war can be traced to Eris, the goddess of discord. She resented the harmony enjoyed by her heavenly sisters and decided to stir up trouble between them. She contacted the god Zeus and asked him to judge "a beauty contest" and select the most beautiful goddess in the heavens. Zeus had misgivings about the request, fearing that favoring one goddess would jeopardize other potential female conquests. So he arranged for Paris, a modest shepherd who was deemed the most honest man in the kingdom, to be his stand-in. Paris had to choose between Aphrodite, Hera, and Athena. The designated beauty would win the golden apple of discord. You'd think the name of that apple should have given something away, but, as we all know, vanity can rob us of our common sense. Paris deemed Aphrodite the winner. As a sign of gratitude, she arranged to give Paris the most beautiful mortal woman in the land. Unfortunately, this particular woman, Helen, was married. This did not go over well with the kingdom of Sparta, and eventually, the conflict unleashed the Trojan War.

You might be surprised to learn that the woman whose face "launched a thousand ships," was a size fourteen. Helen, with the lovely face and ample frame, excited the entire world and plunged countless men into war. Some historians depict her as a willing participant in the legendary saga. Others describe Helen as a faithful wife who was unwillingly snatched from the arms of her husband and children. This is what I think: Paris was Helen's chance to grab the brass ring and enjoy a little adventure in her life. Her marriage had probably been arranged by her father, and the children she bore were the result of an obligation to fulfill her "wifely duties." Meanwhile, honorable Paris had been groomed by Aphrodite. Surely, the wise goddess wouldn't have chosen Helen as the world's most beautiful mortal woman if Paris hadn't been worthy of the reward.

Helen is one example of the voluptuous femme fatales whose stories can be found in the history of the ancient world. They were women who had form and substance. Read about them and bring your own interpretation to the tales, challenge the male viewpoint and draw new conclusions. Most of all, use their lives to inspire your own.

Would you care to indulge me in a new spin on witches? Circe—whose hair was said to resemble flames—was one tough lady. She sat, perched on a throne, wearing a purple robe and a golden veil. She had the voice of an angel but the attitude of the most manipulative, cunning demon. Once, when a lover betrayed her, she turned him into a pig. Casting her spell, Circe recited, "Be as your nature." Imagine, if we had that power, how much easier it would be to find a worthy man. At the very least, there'd be more bacon frying in the skillet.

Another ancient lady of power we should draw strength from comes right from the Bible. Before Eve took a bite from the forbidden apple, Lilith was the first woman to reside in the Garden of Eden. She was placed on earth to become Adam's equal. She was so equal, in fact, that she was literally the other side of Adam—more specifically, the back side, and so Adam possessed male and female attributes. God realized that this was probably not the best way to procreate and make the world plentiful. So he put Adam to sleep and separated Lilith from his body. After further refinement, God dressed Lilith as a radiant bride and then presented her to Adam, proud of the perfect match he had created. There was one major problem. Adam recoiled from Lilith's independent nature. In fairness, it was probably tough for Adam to wake up and find that his "better half" was, in fact, his other half. He desired a woman who would be subservient, someone who would bow down and adore him—and never give him any shit. Lilith wanted no part of playing the demure little lady. God was a little confused Himself. He wondered if a better balance could be found by giving Adam a woman who would look up to him. Since God refused to defend Lilith, and her radical beliefs, she split the scene and escaped from Eden.

This is the way I see it: Lilith was the original emancipated woman. She had bigger, and better, things to do with her time. Her departure did not sit so well with Adam, or, according to male historians, with God either. Basically, Adam didn't want Lilith, and he didn't want her to find fulfillment elsewhere. He wanted to control her, setting the stage for thousands of years of male domination.

Meanwhile, Lilith's reputation took a beating. She was dubbed the queen of demons. Interestingly, Adam went the extra step and claimed Lilith was frigid. Imagine the absurdity of that depiction: a seductress who's also frigid. Basically, Lilith, this strong, independent woman, existed as men defined her, and all because she bucked the system.

In time, men swore that Lilith tormented them in their sleep. They claimed she seduced them by appearing uninvited in their dreams. She was also called night monster. A rabbi actually forbade men to sleep alone so that they wouldn't become Lilith's prey. I'll bet there were some jealous wives lurking in the background, putting undue influence on the rabbi. Not only did this beguiling babe have her way when they were asleep, she messed with them while they were awake. Bewitched men had a habit of getting it on with other women.

As for the claim that it was all Lilith's fault, that she led these men down the garden path of forbidden pleasure, I don't think they needed any encouragement. Have you ever met a man who needed more than a wink of the eye, a turn of the head, or an unseemly glance at exposed cleavage to begin his own dance of seduction? I think our problems can all be traced to Adam's superego. Lilith's brain was as supple as her body. She left Adam salivating at the altar. Adam, who unknowingly positioned himself as the prototype for the typical male, could not stand her rejection. After he got drunk with the snake, he decided to malign our Lilith so that he could save his own reputation as a great lover. If Eve had been given the straight scoop about Adam, and his sexual deficiencies, I'll bet she would have followed Lilith straight out of Eden and used their combined powers to influence other men who were more worthy partners.

Another group of lusty ladies who should be admired and respected are those voluptuous goddesses of the sea, mermaids. These glorious creatures inhabited the oceans, occasionally allowing a homesick sailor a glimpse of an iridescent tail, a bared breast, and a welcoming smile. They glided through the waters with grace and ease as their wet, tangled hair streamed seductively down their backs. Singing the mournful tunes of lost love, these water spirits would capture the gaze of a seaman, stretch their arms toward him, and plead that he join them for a life of eternal love. These beauties were the epitome of eroticism and few could resist the promises they offered.

The gals of old England were a bit more reserved. In days of old, when men were bold, there lived in Camelot a fair maiden named Guinevere. A Welsh princess, her breasts were said to resemble ripe, succulent melons always straining against their bodice. Her belly was rounded and her hips were made for bearing children. We're not talking Calista Flockhart, ladies. Guinevere, this goddess of flowers and light, had men waiting in line for her. Sir Lancelot and King Arthur both desired Guinevere's hand. Poor Guinevere, what a decision. On the one hand, we have the debonair king: tall, handsome, rich, with long, black, silky hair and eyes the color of coal. (He also scored points because he had his own kingdom.) On the other hand, we have the dashing Sir Lancelot. Gorgeous! Huge in the chest and shoulders, long muscular legs, eyes the deepest of blue and blond, curly hair that swept the center of his rippling back. Whenever Guinevere watched him ride in on his trusty steed, the nectar from her petals would run down her thighs, or so it has been said. This man definitely lit up her pleasure zone.

But finally, after much contemplation, Guinevere realized she had to look out for number one and chose riches over love, prestige over lust, Arthur over Lancelot. Let's face it, ladies, what girl could resist her own kingdom? Arthur was giddy with his conquest even though Merlin the magician had warned him that he was asking for trouble—big trouble. But Arthur didn't listen. When have men ever listened to reason? So the marriage was celebrated throughout the kingdom of Camelot, and for a while the marriage bed was pure if not very exciting.

Then, Sir Meliagraunce, a knight desirous of our Guinevere, arrived on the scene and took matters into his own hands. One dark night, Meliagraunce crept into the castle and kidnapped Guinevere. Since this was a woman who didn't lose sight of her advantages, she allowed herself to be seduced. Remember, in those days, if you wanted to get out of a bad relationship, it was not just a matter of finding the car keys and hitting the gas pedal. She made the best of a bad situation, and it worked out for a while. Fortunately, just when our lady was getting bored, Lancelot appeared on the scene to rescue his lost love. And you thought the plots developed for soap operas were too convenient.

King Arthur, out of his mind with grief and worry, and not thinking too clearly, called upon his old rival for assistance. Big mistake. Remember Merlin's warning? Guinevere and Lancelot fell irrevocably in love. Though their renewed passion made them feel guilty, they could not bear the thought of separation, which did not go down well with poor Arthur. He was rejected romantically. The staggering blow to his heart was like a dagger, to say nothing of the damage to his manhood. This affair, plus an ensuing fight between Arthur and Lancelot, was the catalyst that resulted in the downfall of Camelot.

Do you see a pattern here? Soft women, rounded women, women who never knew what a crash diet was, who never went under the scalpel of a plastic surgeon, women with bodies as nature intended them; these are the women who have driven men to fight wars. Men have groveled at their feet, begged for their love, and sacrificed their own lives for these full-figured heroines.

I can't think of any scrawny stick women being held up as a banner for womanhood anywhere in the past. And what 100-pound pioneer woman could have survived the prairie after crossing the country in a covered wagon? It makes you realize that the phrase, "the closer to the bone, the sweeter the meat," is a complete fallacy—a fairy tale created by some marketing genius on Madison Avenue who had a warehouse of preshrunk designer jeans he needed to unload.

It's amazing how easily the great events and people of the past are forgotten. Historically, mythically, religiously, artistically—we big women have been adored by men of every century. Why not now? Should we chalk it up as a fad, and trust that our popularity will come around again? Okay, I can buy that. Should we say that men have lost their brains? I can definitely buy that. But maybe we can tell ourselves that our beauty, confidence, and sensuality intimidates the world too much for men to admit.

Or maybe we should just bring back the Amazon society and put an end to all the crap.

15

Sexy Power and Play

Even if we aren't consciously aware of it, we've all, at one time or another, used sex to get what we wanted. It goes back to childhood, when we were "Daddy's little girl." We wanted to have things our way, and we figured Daddy was the quickest route to making it happen.

To fool my mother, manipulation was something I learned as a kid in order to survive. Since I never knew when I was considered good or bad—or, for that matter, when I'd get popped up side the head—I manipulated my emotions and adapted different roles that would go straight to the heart of Dad. Eventually, it spilled over into my interaction with other adults and even my fellow classmates at school. Subconsciously, it has occasionally carried over into my sex life.

When simply asking for what you want doesn't work, a sexy smile or touch can do wonders to get things out of people. The motivation to manipulate begins with the instinct for self-preservation; once we've accomplished our goal, it becomes a magnificent power trip. I should know; I can be a great manipulator.

For anyone who might think I'm advocating screwing to get what you want, make no mistake: There's a clear distinction between flirtation and actually trading sex for favors. I'm all for flirtation, but trading sex for favors comes at a potentially terrible price. We cannot allow our bodies to be exploited by someone who wouldn't otherwise give us what we wanted. Though a man's goal is sexual gratification, he walks away with far more into the bargain: He takes our power. Meanwhile, because we wouldn't want anything to do with the guy, we've not only given that power away, we've also lost some self-esteem and possibly the promotion, too, because we've lost his professional respect.

When I was younger, there were periods when I was losing weight and, wouldn't you know it, I found my dance card full. I'd be on a date, having a grand old time, behaving like the belle of the ball. When the night ended, my date usually wanted—and actually expected—sex. Even if I wasn't comfortable with the idea, I somehow felt responsible, as if I had teased him or led him on and now I was obligated to put out. Many of us have found ourselves backed into that corner; too often we submitted to the pressure just because we didn't want to make a scene or have the guy think we were frigid or a tease. It took many long hours of self-examination and reflection for me to finally understand that anytime you allow someone to have his way because you felt responsible for his urges, you've given up your power; and under those circumstances, there is no way that sex can possibly be fulfilling.

The fascinating and wonderful thing about being a woman today is that we can learn from our past, and move boldly forward, free of the shackles that once determined how we defined ourselves sexually. By understanding our power, we can steer the course of our own sexual lives, unencumbered by male manipulation or society's expectations.

My mother had an expression for flirting: "catting around." The implication was that you were like a cat in heat, driven by your insatiable desire to have sex. Since you had no control over your wanton urges, there were safety precautions that good girls should take. Before going on a date, you didn't shave your legs. You also wore Grandma's bloomers (not literally, just the style). The theory was that you'd feel so awful about yourself that you wouldn't dare let a man get close. Of course, a girlfriend has told me that European men are not repelled by hairy armpits or legs. In fact, an African American friend also told me that she didn't shave her legs because her husband liked them fuzzy. As for Grandma's bloomers, they can come off just as easily as they're put on. Let's face it, if you're on a date and your mind-set is, "This is gonna happen tonight!", Grandma's undies are gonna get tossed in the nearest Dumpster.

The bottom line is, there are occasions when lust takes precedence and kitty has to be satisfied—we experience primal, animalistic attractions just the same as those of men. On my first date with Rolf, after he had already seen me prancing around half naked onstage and had whipped my lost panty hose out of his pocket, the last thing I thought about was spending the night at his place. It happened. But what Mom's generation called "catting around" I prefer to think of as "the kitten factor."

Of course, being able to act on our lusty desires means that we need to be extra diligent in understanding our response afterward. Many guys are perfectly comfortable fulfilling their physical desires and moving on; it's how society has conditioned them to behave. It's far more common for women's fulfilled lust to evolve into deeper feelings, and when that happens, you absolutely must address it. If one person is feeling love and the other is experiencing plain old lust, the relationship will never work. Someone's bound to get hurt, and it's usually the woman.

On the flip side, when women withhold acting on lust—in hopes that their "one and only" is just around the corner—wonderful opportunities can pass them by. After all, the experiences we gain in our single years can help us reap luscious benefits once we settle down and marry. Trust me, though your husband may not want specific names and dates, he'll be very appreciative of the boudoir expertise you bring into the marriage.

There are those treasured, blissful occasions when the heat of the moment is perfect and you're both in sync and loving each wild, pulsating moment. But, inevitably, there will be more occasions when he makes it to the finish line while you're still at the starting gate. While you lie there and wonder, "Where's mine?", he's already fast asleep and probably snoring. Ladies, here's the brutal truth: We are responsible for our own orgasms.

Now that you've recovered from that earth-shattering revelation, it's time we get to the solution. Would you like to know the best, single investment you could ever make in your life? It costs less than a hundred bucks. It's a multipurpose piece of equipment that works wonders on your tight neck muscles, back pains, and all those beautiful erogenous zones you've heard other women talk about, but will now discover for yourself. It's called a vibrator.

So grab your Yellow Pages and turn to the section titled "Books— Retail." Scan the pages for adult bookstores that advertise novelty products. If you're uneasy about going alone, maybe you could call a fun-loving girlfriend and make the shopping trip an adventure.

But you don't necessarily have to trek over to an adult bookstore. (But wouldn't it be a kick to count how many male neighbors you find skulking in the magazine section?) In the same section of the Yellow Pages, you can usually find stores listed that sell a variety of fascinating products (for instance, fur-lined handcuffs). In Los Angeles, there are shops such as The Pleasure Chest and Drake's. You can feel anonymous standing among the thrill-seeking, middle-America tourists, and maybe even spot a celebrity. Pamela Anderson, Don Johnson, and Madonna are among the stars who have been sighted at such stores, captured in "Gotcha!" tabloid photos, stocking up on products.

If you prefer not to shop in person, there are other alternatives. Flip through the back pages of such benign magazines as *US Weekly* and *Esquire,* and you'll find ads for mail-order stores that specialize in erotica. For the computer savvy, try an Internet search engine such as Google or Yahoo and enter "erotica" as the key word and you're sure to find many on-line stores. Find out if the store ships its products wrapped in brown paper wrapping, with a discreet return address that doesn't scream, "You just bought a vibrator!" That way, there won't be any need to feel embarrassed about the mailman leaving your new wonder toy at your doorstep.

You probably know women who wouldn't approve of owning a vibrator. They're probably the same women who have never experienced an orgasm. Their harsh judgment doesn't have to discourage you. We're not talking about planning a PTA bake sale; this is about buying a vibrator. Remember—and I can't emphasize this enough—what you choose to do with your body is no one else's business. Relax and enjoy yourself.

Your new toy, just like men, comes in all shapes, sizes, and colors. It can operate by batteries or electricity. Personally, I prefer the deluxe, 120-volt-plug-it-into-the-wall-socket-and-fly-yourself-to-the-moon model. Once you've revved up your toy, you'll discover the pleasures you've been missing.

It's not unusual that a woman's first reaction to self-pleasure is guilt. My friend Sue now laughs about the first vibrator she bought. She plugged it into a wall socket and then . . . massaged her shoulders. She swears she didn't even think of putting it anywhere else. After a few weeks, the kinks in Sue's neck were straightened out, so she wondered what her vibrator would feel like on other parts of her body.

Sue discovered it felt quite pleasant on her breasts, her inner thighs, and, eventually, her inner Netherlands. It was a bonding experience; she was so delighted with her vibrator that she named it Joe. Before long, Sue recounts, with Joe around she didn't need a man to experience an orgasm. In fact, what took her boyfriend half an hour to accomplish only took minutes with Joe. Sue thought Joe might be a good influence on her boyfriend. With Joe taking the lead, Sue hoped her boyfriend would learn how she enjoyed her body being touched and caressed. But when Sue introduced Joe to her boyfriend, all hell broke loose. Her boyfriend was outraged by Joe's presence. Behaving like, well, a jealous lover, he called Sue a perverted nymphomaniac and demanded that she toss Joe into the trash. Amused by her boyfriend's childish outburst, Sue refused; he stormed out, never to be seen again. Ever practical, Sue didn't miss him. You see, her boyfriend could give her only one orgasm, while Joe specialized in multiple orgasms. With a wicked smile, Sue likes to remark, "I think it was penis envy." Though Sue has moved on to other boyfriends—and vibrators—Joe enjoys a permanent place in her dresser's bottom drawer. Unlike Sue's insecure boyfriend, Joe never walked out on her.

If you still feel uncomfortable about bringing toys into the bedroom, you can try exploring your body with your hands. You'll soon develop techniques that, with well-placed strokes and rhythms, will stimulate you to the Big O. Later, you might even share with your boyfriend the fact that hands and the tongue can be just as satisfying, maybe even more pleasure-giving, as his penis.

On a humorous note, let me tell you about a friend who took her Big O on the road. She was driving from Los Angeles to Vegas. While cruising through the desert, she found the long, empty stretch of road monotonous. With no one else around, she took one hand from the steering wheel and nestled it between her thighs. She soon lost sense of her speed. In her rearview mirror, she noticed a traffic cop appear on his motorcycle, lights flashing. The chase only intensified her pleasure. Teetering on the brink of orgasm, she decided, "Screw the ticket, I'm almost there!" She continued driving until she was making sounds like Meg Ryan in *When Harry Met Sally*. Finally, satiated, she steered her car to the shoulder of the road and stopped. When the traffic cop approached her, she claimed she hadn't noticed his lights. My friend was convinced the officer had his suspicions about the real reason she was unable stop, because her breathing was rapid and heavy. She paid the ticket. But I've always been convinced that had she gone to court and challenged the ticket, she could have beaten the charges—provided she had a female judge.

My grandmother, bless her soul, may she rest in peace, was 101 years old when she shared with me her concern that she might have married the wrong man. When I asked why, she answered in a matter-of-fact way that it was their sex life. Grandpa would just climb on top of her, and when he was satisfied, he rolled off and fell fast asleep. "What else was there?" she inquired. I told Grandma that masturbation was a good alternative and that we had to buy her a vibrator. She had no idea what I was talking about and shyly asked what kind of vibrator would have anything to do with sex, and then, how to use it. It saddens me that she went through life with a "Wham-bam-thank-you-mam!" husband who never once thought about satisfying her needs. The bigger tragedy is, because of the times, Grandma never realized she could satisfy herself. When she was a young woman, brides were virgins who were to serve and obey their husbands without question or any thought to their own sexual needs. Even talking to her friends would not have helped because they knew nothing either. I felt privileged that she trusted me, her granddaughter, with intimate details of her marriage and sexual curiosity. I'm sure she never had conversations like we did with my mom or uncle. Think of how far we've come: Women talk freely about their sexual adventures; and when we want to be anonymous, we can go to any number of websites for answers to our most intimate and formerly embarrassing questions.

In Los Angeles, strip clubs are part of the quirky landscape, along with buildings bizarrely shaped, like a doughnut or a hot dog. The clubs have goofy names like Star Strip and The Body Shop. (Curiously, across the nation, strip joints are usually found in close proximity to the local airport—I guess there's something about flying that makes the male libido crave a lap dance.) We could get huffy, because some dentally challenged chick named Tammy Sue is shaking her silicone-implanted oversize bazookas in our hubby's salivating face, or we can do something about it. My motto is: Why go out when there's a better floor show at home?

Stripping for Rolf is something that I eased into gradually. After all, who among us nonprofessionals can just dive in and get it right the first time? Picture the probable scenario. A husband arrives home and finds his wife, in wild abandon, doing a pole dance on the bedpost. He'll start looking under the bed for an empty vodka bottle.

First, try taking baby steps. Purchase two sexy pairs of panties. (For you shy ones, isn't on-line shopping wonderful?) Place them in a perfume-scented envelope and attach a handwritten note that reads: "Honey, I bought these just for you. When you get home tonight, I'll be wearing the blue ones." It creates anticipation, allowing you and your husband to enjoy the fantasy while slowly playing out the sweet scenario.

By all means, experiment. Put different types of music in the CD player. Dim the bedroom lights. Maybe even keep the bedroom shades slightly open. Find what works for both of you. Perhaps you could coax him into doing it. Think of the pleasure you'll both have in sharing the experience together.

Believe me, I know that because of the insecurities we have about our bodies—especially those of us who are beyond size fourteen—undressing for a lover can be intimidating. So, before doing anything, it's important that you feel absolutely 100 percent comfortable. Otherwise, walls go up immediately and the opportunity for fun and intimacy is lost. If you're afraid that his response will be, "What the hell's gotten into you today?", try beginning with a milder approach to entice him. Maybe a bra that snaps off quickly while you're preparing for bed will grab his attention. His response is a safe way to determine how much further you want to take things the next time.

Think of the possibilities his wallet, or a book that he's reading, holds for your amorous desires. Slip a naughty note into it that begins with these five words, "I want you to lick . . ." After the initial shock wears off, he'll probably arrive home primed to perform. With the sexual tension that's built during his workday, you won't even have time to strip, because he'll undo your clothes faster than you can.

If being a little naughty is something new for you, communication can help to protect against surprise responses that might feel hurtful. For instance, movies can be a wonderful springboard to initiate conversations about intimacy. Try to recall a movie from your dating days that might have led to hot and heavy petting in the backseat of his car. Next, find out if it's available at your nearest video rental place. When he gets home, slip it into the VCR or DVD player and watch his reaction. Take him back to those days when passion drove everything in your relationship. Ask what was it about you that turned him on. Share with him the things that turned you on. Find out if there were any secret fantasies he played in his mind about you. It's possible that the discussion will create ideas for a future seduction, or, ideally, end in bed that night, making love.

Slowly undressing a man is fantastic foreplay. He enjoys the attention you're showing him. As women, we, of course, need to know our own bodies, but it's also important to know his body, and to understand how he reacts to stimuli. Granted, a lot of times all you have to do is whisper in his ear and he's up and ready to go. But we're not interested in your average, garden-variety jackrabbit. We want the Energizer bunny, who just keeps going and going. By undressing your man—slowly—you learn the little things that bring him up, and what you can do to bring him down again. Maybe it's the way you loosen his tie, how you unbutton his shirt, or where you move your hands when they're in his pants pockets. For that particular move, I like to lean forward and whisper in my husband's ear, "My hand is the squirrel and it's looking for nuts."

Hey, whatever starts your motor purring.

16

A Little Bit Kinky

When Rolf and I dated, back in the wild '70s, we rented a motel room that had a waterbed and a sunken tub. If I remember right, it was a "rent-by-the-hour" room. The lascivious look I got from the check-in clerk made me feel absolutely wicked. I wish I had had a stick of gum in my mouth, so that I could really look the part of a "working girl." Rolf and I had so much fun on that waterbed, and the sunken tub gave new meaning to the phrase "taking a bath."

The bathroom held an unexpected surprise: a bidet, which resembles a small toilet, except the water gently sprays upward. Europeans have them in their bathrooms for hygienic cleaning after you've finished your usual activities. You can also find them at several New Orleans hotels. Now, use your imagination and picture what you can do with a bidet and that wonderful spray. I'm sure any Frenchwoman could give you a few good pointers. But be forewarned: If you're visiting France, or New Orleans, as a tourist, it will take great restraint to get yourself out of that bathroom.

I studied with an acting coach who taught techniques for acting in commercials. Turns out that wasn't all she taught. She recommended that I get a Water Pik and a shower-massage head. I made the purchases and took them home. Later, I mentioned that I didn't understand what the big deal was. She told me, "If you don't know, then you're not using them the right way." Later, I discovered exactly what she met. It's amazing what turning a nozzle in a certain direction can do. Let's just say, my water bill that month saw a tremendous increase. But I was also "fresh as a spring rain."

Talking with your lover about pleasuring yourself can be a major turn-on. With my role on *Days of Our Lives*, I frequently travel. Meanwhile, poor Rolf's home alone. Growing up, we're taught that masturbation is wrong. Adolescent boys often have wet dreams, but they're told that if they give in to temptation when they're awake, they'll go blind, or hair will grow on their palms. It's unfortunate that we're taught that masturbation is a shameful thing. It's actually a natural way to explore your body. Sharing your feelings about it can build intimacy in your relationship.

Putting a condom on your lover with your hands is one thing. But doing it with your mouth is something every woman should learn. Get a banana, get a condom, and practice putting the darn thing on. Think how exciting it would be for him to see you doing it or, better yet, feel you doing it.

Instead of running to the bathroom to put in your diaphragm, make it a team effort. If you're embarrassed to have him help you with your diaphragm, consider the other things you've done together. It's fun to learn about each other's bodies. You're usually as naked as a jaybird while having sex. Would it really be that difficult to have him participate in helping with your diaphragm? You might be surprised; men actually want to know about that mysterious process. Next time you're at the grocery store, check the sexual surveys in men's magazines. Granted, a woman has the right to keep certain secrets from a man, but this doesn't have to be one of them.

In some states, sodomy is actually against the law. Well, excuse me, but there are a lot of people who like that stuff. If it's not hurting anyone, what's the problem? I have a friend whose husband is really into that type of intimacy. Initially, it was a problem for her because it felt painful. But she's learned to relax, and now enjoys it every once in a while. (As for me, nothing goes in the back door. I can't even take a finger there when the doctor does my complete gynecological exam.) Curiously, my friend said that even though it was a painful thing for her, she liked the pain. I have to emphasize that any kind of sexual encounter must be enjoyed by both participants. Ladies, don't do anything that hurts you or makes you feel uncomfortable. Talk it over with your mate.

For you women who are unsure, I have heard through another girlfriend that anal sex is worth the initial discomfort, especially when her partner massages her clitoris at the same time. She tells me her orgasms pack a double dose of dynamite. Also, there are a large number of heterosexual men who enjoy back-side stimulation because it's near the prostate, which is at the base of the penis. Slight pressure in that area just behind the testicles, and in front of the other end, can be very pleasurable for a man. If you're willing to explore, you might want to try it. But be gentle—men can be so delicate.

I don't think the English language has a word that aptly describes the "Aaahhhh!" moment. As I've mentioned, I have been married a long time, and wasn't too experienced beforehand. I am very lucky to have somebody who wants to playfully "slap and tickle" me all the time and be adventurous. But I think there would be a lot more playful slap and tickling if we all felt comfortable communicating, and didn't allow ourselves to be repressed by society's rules about what's proper and what isn't.

I still vividly remember my first orgasm. Who doesn't? I didn't understand exactly what was happening with my body but, now, when it finally starts, I know that I'm taking a trip down the happy trail. The bottom line is this: If he gets done before me, he better wait until I'm done, and even help me down that trail. And if he can't muster up the energy to do that, he better not get upset when I walk into the other room and whip out the vibrator, or reach down and handle the joy button myself.

We've all heard about multiple orgasms. There are women who have gone so long without ever experiencing it, or have never experienced it, that they think it's a myth. Other women will tell you they have more than one orgasm all the time with their lovers. I've also heard my friends say you should be happy if you have just one, because that's more than most women get. I'm sorry, but I disagree. Sure, it's nice to achieve one Big O, but it's even better to enjoy multiples. If your man could have more than one at a time, you'd never hear him say, "Be happy with that one bang!" By the way, I have heard of men achieving multiple orgasms, too, and they're not in their twenties. More than one girlfriend has told me about lovers who are orgasmic three to six times in a ninety-minute time frame, without losing their erection for more than a few minutes. It tells me that practice, exploration, and an open mind can bring rich rewards.

I won't lie. Like a lot of women, I have faked it. But I've found that I'm not comfortable pretending; I just don't like to do that. Not only do I feel cheated, I feel like I'm doing the same to my lover. Instead of carrying unnecessary guilt, I'd rather use the time to communicate and be intimate. Although I admit that there are also those times when I just want him to get off and go away. Sometimes a man may feel the same way, so you'll be surprised to find that there's not always a lot of resistance to taking care of your own business.

If my lover didn't have an orgasm, I'd think that there was something physically wrong. Men are generally going to have one, regardless. Unless, of course, there is a real problem. Let's face it, men have a different mind-set. I have often heard men say, "There's no such thing as a bad fuck," or, "I've never met a naked woman I didn't like." As most women know, men can often leave their emotions at the door.

I'm sure men think it's very crucial to reach orgasm. But I suspect that's the whole ego thing about a) not getting it up, b) not keeping it up, and c) nothing happening. When that happens to a man, he's going to think he's no longer a man. I'm sure that's pretty traumatic, especially if you just met, and it's your first, or second, date. Both parties can feel pretty disappointed. The woman's thinking, "Well, that's it for him," and he's fretting, "She's going to tell all her friends!"

On the other hand, if you have time invested in the relationship and something does happen, it's important to be supportive. Stress and inhibition can interfere with male performance. Ask him if he's feeling okay, or if he's stressed out. Maybe he lost a bundle betting on *Monday Night Football*. I've seen that disrupt plenty of relationships—if his team's not scoring, he's not scoring, and that means you're going to get shut out. If it is an emotional issue, then talk it out. If it's physical, get him to the doctor. Who knows? Maybe he'll get a prescription for Viagra or a consultation with a psychologist. In any case, communicate.

I've heard women boast that they've climaxed horseback riding, or while driving on a bumpy road. I think that's absolutely fantastic, if it's true. My friends tell me that the best part is keeping it a secret. It becomes a bigger moment; there is the mystery of sitting there, having it, and not letting anyone know. A hot tub in the yard or a spa tub in the bathroom can be fun. Those well-placed jets sending powerful surges of water can—when you find the right position—

help you have delightful gushes of your own. I've also been told that sitting on the washer while it's on the spin cycle gives you an extra-special kick. Yes, I've tried it, and I'm here to say that I have never felt the same about laundry since. I probably have the cleanest laundry on the block. Whatever works, enjoy it.

Another public place that allows for crazy climaxes is clubs. It has to do with the bass sound. It vibrates everything inside you. When I worked in the music business, I'd go to clubs often and there would be a big, loud bass sound running directly under the benches. I'm willing to bet the sound people do all of this on purpose. People sit there, wondering why they are feeling the way they are, every part of their body tingling. Next time you're in a club, say a silent "Thank you" to the soundman. Once I had dinner, drinks, and four orgasms, all while sitting in a club. That tingling primed for that fifth one, at home, with Rolf.

My husband gets attention from women all the time, mostly from my single girlfriends. They call up and say they need him to fix the water faucet, or help them move something. As thanks, they'll invite both of us over for dinner. When I can't make it, I tell him to go without me and have a good time. It's all about trust and talking to each other. There's no aphrodisiac in the world more powerful than a trusting relationship.

If both partners are willing and wanting, I say push the envelope and go for the fantasy. If you like real police handcuffs and mean serious business, go for it. Personally, I prefer the less painful cuffs made out of faux fur.

When you give your partner a massage, or he's giving you one, you probably use fragrant oil. Here's a suggestion: Heat the oil to a nice warm—but not hot—degree. It's almost guaranteed to add moans of pleasure to the sensual experience.

Feathers are another fun, yet painless, toy I like sometimes. You could try using single feathers, of different shapes or sizes. Then, alternate with several feathers at once. Frankly, it's a tickle I just can't get with anything else!

Though I have no problem playing Daisy Duck with the feathers, or slathering my body so that I glisten like a French fry, there is one role I can't see myself playing: a dominatrix. Although there are occasions when I enjoy being in control, I doubt I'd enjoy dominating anyone. However, I'm not going to condemn anyone who does like that sort of thing. Whatever makes you feel good in the privacy of your own bedroom is nobody's business but your own. As long as both partners agree, it doesn't hurt anyone, and no innocent farm animals are injured in the process, let the games begin.

17

Fashion and Style

What we wear tells the world how we want to be treated and how we feel about ourselves. Clothes and attitude make up my personal style, which I'd describe as "out there." Not wacky, or weird out there, but vibrant and bold. So I choose clothes and colors that express a bright and cheerful outlook.

I learned to sew from my mom and grandmother while still in grammar school. Nice clothes in larger sizes weren't as easy to find back then, so I often made skirts, blouses, and dresses for myself. I learned to alter patterns that didn't come in larger sizes, too. This helped when I sewed clothes for theater productions where not everyone was the same size. Heck, I even sewed drapes and pillow and furniture covers, too.

A few years ago, I was browsing through a vintage-clothing store when a party dress caught my eye. I liked the style, which was very flamboyant. I purchased the dress, took it apart, and redesigned the material to create a contemporary look. When I wore it to a Hollywood event, I discovered that the material was very clingy, which made me self-conscious because it was hugging my body. I felt uncomfortable the entire night. I also wore a gorgeous shawl. By the end of the evening, the shawl was no longer a fashion accessory. It had become my security blanket.

When I returned home, I thought about why I had hidden behind the shawl, and I realized that my discomfort had nothing to do with the dress. I felt awkward being in my own skin. If I had to wear the dress as Nancy on *Days of Our Lives*, I wouldn't have thought twice about it; I would have been focused on my work. After all, Patrika wasn't wearing the dress, the costume designer selected it for Nancy, a fictitious character on a soap.

At the event, though, I was me, Patrika Darbo, star of *Days of Our Lives*, and throughout the evening photographers snapped my picture. Eventually, the photos would surface in the soap magazines or possibly in the tabloids. When I attended the Daytime Emmys last year, I wore a fabulous blue outfit. A week later, my picture was on the cover of *The Star*. It was also featured in a spread about the Daytime Emmys in a soap magazine. The caption read, "What was she thinking with those shoes?"

When you attend show-business events, you're expected to be perfect at all times. It's ridiculous. Some stars stand in a frozen pose the entire night. They want to look good because they expect to see themselves in magazines. Meanwhile, I mingle, laugh, raise my arms, twist and turn. I'm too busy having fun to act like a statue. But being animated means there's a chance I might be captured in an awkward pose, and, boy, do the tabloids love awkward poses. It makes stars look foolish, which enables the editors to feel superior. Admittedly, when I see photos of myself with a snarky caption, I'll sometimes agree. But at the time the photo was shot, I was having a great time.

Although I'm plus-size, I'm also under five feet, three inches. Some stores put clothes for my height in the petite section.

Unfortunately, the height is rarely considered in conjunction with a full figure. My body is shaped like a lightbulb. Most designers create clothes for a woman whose body resembles a pear. Therefore, when I buy a dress, it's snug enough at the top to strangle my boobs. Meanwhile, the material at the bottom is wide enough to dress two people. So I mix and match my clothes.

On *Days of Our Lives,* we had to take unusual measures with a pants suit I wore in one episode. In order for the crotch to be in the right place, I had to pull the waistband up and hook it to my bra. That's how much extra material was left. Thank goodness there wasn't a photographer around to snap me, showing the waistband hooked to my bra. (I can just imagine the caption I'd read in a tabloid for *that* photo: "*Days of Our Lives* Star Hooked.")

The *Los Angeles Times* once ran a fashion article that chastised clothing designers and stores for overlooking a potentially lucrative market—petite, full-figured women. Stores serve the other end of the market, big and tall, so I don't understand why big and short is ignored. All women, big or not, can find designers, and stores, that fit them best in terms of style and size. You don't have to limit yourself to the one store that sells only navy blue polyester; those days are long gone. If you want to wear something strapless, but prefer not to have body parts hanging out, find something you can adapt, something that makes you feel sexy. It might be a wrap, thicker straps, a choker, or chiffon sleeves. When I feel good in what I'm wearing, my whole attitude changes. That's the vibe that you project to everyone else.

Designer Carol Little always cuts full-size. When I am below two hundred pounds, I can generally wear her size sixteen. I also wear quite a bit of Liz Claiborne's plus-size line, Elizabeth. If I get a top, it will go to my knees because I'm not five feet, eight inches. But her petite line comes to midlength on me, which is the perfect fit, especially in sports clothes. So if designers are making sexy clothes in our size, by all means support them. Buy the clothes, and wear them.

When I'm feeling blue, like most women I know, I head straight for the mall. I love to shop. A shoe store is a very happy place for me. If a new pair of shoes catches my eye, I'm as excited as a kid on her way to Disneyland. No matter what my weight is, I can always find shoes that fit. Rare is the day I leave a shopping mall without several shoe boxes tucked beneath my arms. If my mood still requires lifting, I'll even buy matching handbags. It's a concept Rolf can't grasp: buying shoes and matching handbags to brighten your mood. With, or without, a fabulous new pair of shoes, when I want to look, and feel, my best, I hold my shoulders back while my breasts stand at attention, proudly saluting the world. It does wonders for my attitude, and my spine.

My wardrobe includes shorts, tights, and several pairs of Capri slacks, which gives the impression that I'm taller. A soap fashion magazine editor once asked, "Are Capri slacks all she has in her closet?" Yes, it's my signature outfit.

When it comes to colors, I believe brighter is better. When I was growing up, there was nothing available in my size except black and navy blue polyester. I spent the swinging sixties with chafed thighs; the scratchy polyester rubbed them raw. I've noticed an attempt by clothing designers to revive polyester, but I'm sticking to cotton. I don't care how much time I spend ironing, or the endless trips to the dry cleaner, I refuse to suffer through another day in polyester.

Though my preference in colors leans toward bright and bold, I'm also drawn to black. It is a staple color. But there's a way to wear black and a way not to. Sometimes black, or navy blue, is slimming and can make us feel comfortable. But you can tell when you're making a sleek fashion statement rather than hiding in a dress that looks like a dark cloud. If you're *hiding* in black, what you're telling people is that you feel so insecure you want to just fade into the background and not be noticed. If you've been teased about your weight, complexion, height (too tall or too short), or anything else that was not "average," hiding can be a habit of self-preservation and protection that you learned in your younger days. You are more mature now and have more control over other people's attitudes and responses, so come out of hiding and enjoy yourself.

If you're not ready to step out in bright-colored or print fashions, start with small changes. To personalize your dark ensemble, you can add bold-colored accessories. Bright colors celebrate life. Adjust your attitude about basic black and be a diva, not a quivering, frightened shadow. Life is too short; whatever package you come in, put a bow on it and live!

Appearing on *Days of Our Lives* has also helped me to appreciate the wonderful things you can do with cosmetics. The makeup department has introduced me to products I wouldn't otherwise have used in my personal life. I experiment more freely in applying eyelashes, glitter shadow, and creams. Once you get it down, it's fun. When you have time, sit and experiment with the eyelash singles. You've got to have patience, but the results are worth it. You can create a natural look with singles. Once you've attached them, work with a fill-in pencil or liquid liner. You will be amazed by the difference. When I performed in the burlesque-style revue *Bottoms Up,* I stuck together three pairs of eyelashes for my top lids and two pairs on the bottom. My eyes looked as big as my head. I was the comedienne and played Big Titty Dolly Farton, among other characters, in the skits. I also did several clothed dance routines and a lot of singing. Okay, so many eyelashes might not look as good in a singles bar as they did from the audience, but practice with new cosmetic techniques you've learned from friends. Have fun.

I wear a light coat of lipstick to brighten my face. If you have a hairy upper lip, and you feel self-conscious about it, wax it off. You can have a session at the beauty salon or can try a product at home. It's that easy.

Now, for my most important beauty tip. Wear a smile on your face. It helps you to be happy with who you are. Share your smile, and say hello to people you encounter throughout the day. You'll be surprised by how many return your friendly gesture with a smile. As an actress, I've entertained the possibility that the day will come when having cosmetic work performed might be a viable option. Aging is a challenge for anyone. It reminds us of our mortality. In Hollywood, it also becomes a liability. A close friend recently had a face-lift. Before the doctor consented to performing the surgery, she was required to lose weight and maintain the loss for one year. A face-lift, or any cosmetic surgery, is a personal choice. If you're clear about why you're doing it, more power to you. But be fore-warned: If you're seeking cosmetic surgery as a cure-all, you're des-tined for disappointment. No amount of plastic surgery fixes a neg-ative self-image.

On a daily basis, I continue to work on building my confidence and self-image. Instead of asking myself what part of my body I'd like to hide, I find the part I'd like to highlight. It helps me look at myself in a loving way rather than critically. I no longer tell myself, "Oh, my arms are sagging," or, "I hate my hips." Instead, I'll smile and announce, "Patrika, your breasts look great today!" Then I dive into the closet to find something that accentuates my breasts and helps me to feel good for the entire day. When you start loving yourself, you'll be surprised by how soon you actually say to your-self, "I'm liking what I see!"

The goal is to feel comfortable in your skin. I'm not suggesting you rush out and buy a strapless, low-cut dress today. My hope, and intention, is that you don't use clothes to hide yourself from the world. We may have it a little tougher than most when it comes to finding the right fit, or stores that supply clothes we can wear. But they are out there, and we need to find them. Our relationship with ourselves, and with the people around us, depends on it. Your mission should be to find something that makes you want to fly. I use shoes to express my style and attitude. What will you use?

Finally, we all know people who raise an eyebrow, or purse their lips, when we dress stylishly. They'd prefer us to feel shameful about our size, and hide behind oversize, shapeless moo-moos. It fits the stereotype that big people are sloppy and careless about their appearance. Their snotty judgment is not about us. It has nothing to do with us. It's about them. They're so uptight about what might happen to them if they eat a slice of apple pie that they try to make us feel shame for their secret desires. It's the same principle that applies to women who are sexually active. They're supposed to feel like tramps so that the people pointing fingers never have to examine their own repressed sexual impulses. Remember: It's not what other people think that rules our lives. It's what we think of ourselves.

18

Sexy in Every Season

Spring

MARCH

St. Patrick's Day

Just because the infamous month of love is over doesn't mean our hot
new sex life has to end. After recuperating from a lusty February,
March fills our spirits with reasons to get green. On St. Patrick's Day,
how about kisses for the Irish, and pinches for everyone else? If
you're not Irish, and want a kiss, have a Guinness stout or Shepherd's
pie—become an honorary Irishwoman for a day! Meanwhile, flex
your butt muscles and prepare for those Irish pinches. Rolf and I are
both Irish. Although we don't have a full-blown celebration every
year, there are years when we let our hair down and just have fun.

St. Patrick drove the snakes out of Ireland, which doesn't
exactly evoke a sexy image. However, with sexy thinking, there
are plenty of kinky tips to help your little leprechaun lover find

your pot of gold. Body paint is also available in green, with an assortment of flavors such as mint and lime. You can also splurge and purchase a variety pack to make you look like the rainbow that leads to the pot of gold. You'll also need a bottle of gold body glitter. Your lover can paint a rainbow on you and have it end wherever he'd like to spend the most time on your body. Or paint the rainbow yourself, and have the pot of gold on your favorite spot. (Gold looks great on every skin tone and color, so feel free to skip the green if it's not your best color and make your entire body the pot of gold. But a green body isn't always the most flattering look for some, so be sure to have that gold nearby. I like to highlight those areas I feel need the most sexual attention: nipples, nape of the neck, inner thighs, and toes.) There are wonderful gold-glitter body powders that look terrific in candlelight.

Traditionally, St. Patrick's is a big drinking holiday. Have a few pints of beer—light beer if possible—chilling in an ice bucket. Place it near the bed so it's within reaching distance while your leprechaun digs deep into his pot of gold. If you want to make the hunt for the pot even more exciting, try using golden chocolate coins as a trail across the room and the bed to the pot—you. Tell your little leprechaun that for every coin he finds, he can purchase a special little service, to be delivered later that night, at the end of the rainbow.

APRIL

Easter

Finally! Time for summer dresses comes in April, the month of new beginnings. It's been several months since the overflow of chocolate, but it makes a return on Easter Day. You can easily avoid chocolate by substituting those painted Easter eggs, another sex-energy food. Eggs are loaded with B_5 and B_6 vitamins, which help balance hormones and maintain energy. Believe me, you'll need it for this celebration.

Are you seeing bunny ears? How about a "sex basket" instead of the traditional Easter basket? Easter is definitely one of the best dress-up holidays, since adults associate bunny ears with sex (thanks to our friend Hugh Hefner). You can be a little Easter playmate, with a pair of fuzzy ears and furry panties and bra. Don't forget what rabbits do best, so get your energy up, snacking on a few decorated hard-boiled eggs. Like any holiday full of decorations, this is also a time to write sexy messages on your lover's eggs. You can even send him on an indoor "naked Easter egg hunt." The prize? A cuddly bunny—you! This cute and sexy holiday will make you both laugh out loud at your quirky kinkiness.

Speaking of quirky, when Rolf and I were first married, I told him that the Easter bunny better bring me something. When April arrived, Rolf said that the Easter bunny didn't come to our neck of the woods. I came up with a spontaneous retort: "Then I better see the April walrus!" So, for the first few years of our marriage, he gave me presents from the April walrus. When I stopped insisting on presents from that imaginary friend, he stopped visiting. It wasn't because Rolf loved me any less. It only occurred to him when I reminded him about the April walrus. It was a chore, and he felt pressured—not a good thing. So after a few years, receiving presents from the April walrus wasn't that special because I had to ask for it. This isn't a complaint about my husband; it acknowledges that I understand him. Rolf does really sweet things for me when there's no pressure—when it's not a special occasion or a holiday.

The key to theme seductions is to have fun and a lot of sex. If things haven't been up to par lately, the change of seasons is a perfect opportunity to shake up your love life. Put yourself and your mate in touch with the fresh spring air, the warm sun, and the chirping birds. Let your primal instincts emerge. It's mating season;

catch a serious case of spring fever! If you cannot find a secluded and safe outdoor spot for adult fun, bring the outdoors in with flower-scented candles and oils.

MAY

Memorial Day

You're probably thinking, "How in the world do I equate a patriotic holiday with recharging my sex life?" On Memorial Day, we honor our nation's servicemen who fought in wars so that we could be assured of our freedom. There are plenty of reasons to battle when you're in a marriage or other relationship. How about on this particular day, we make peace, not war? If your husband is in the service or otherwise away, send him a list of all the romantic moments you've shared together; where you can, include photos and souvenirs from those times.

Summer

JUNE

Summer officially arrives on June 21, and the weather becomes so hot that my natural inclination is to stay inside my home all day, where it's air-conditioned. It's the perfect place, and climate, for an all-day turn-on.

If you're not comfortable enough with your body to strut on the beach or poolside in your bathing suit or bikini, I have a suggestion: Wear it under your clothes at work, or around the house if you happen to be home during the day. You'll start to feel confident, and will become familiar with having the suit on while also being really aware of your body. Being aware of your body broadens your opportunities with it, whether it's exercising or massaging yourself. The more you know your body, and are comfortable being in your own skin, the more likely you are to enjoy it and let others receive pleasure from it, too. You can feel like a tropical goddess with a swimsuit and tanning oil on. Oil can make you feel slinky and sexy. You won't be able to keep your hands off yourself!

JULY

Independence Day

Rolf's birthday falls on the fourth of July. So it's a reason to enjoy a double celebration. I used to arrange a big brunch every year. It started out with me calling friends at eight A.M. and saying, "It's a come-as-you-are brunch, get your butts over here, now!" Friends arrived at our door dressed in their pajamas.

It was a madcap time. I'd invite fifty people and seventy-five would show up. People heard it was a great party and wanted to be included. It began at ten A.M. and lasted until three A.M. or until the sun rose. The air-conditioning was set on high, the doors were open, the stoves were burning, and the patio was teeming with festive party guests. Eventually, someone would play the piano, and people gathered around it to sing. They were great parties, combining two celebrations into one event.

As the years passed, though, the guest list got longer and, ultimately, grew out of control. There simply wasn't enough room for people to enjoy themselves. Eventually, Rolf and I decided to stop hosting the brunch. I wanted to spend the time with my husband, celebrating his birthday and enjoying the holiday. Nevertheless, people still showed up at the door, asking, "Isn't the party today?"

If making love isn't like fireworks anymore, you need to set off your own in the bedroom. Pretend you're Lady Liberty and rediscover the glory of sexual freedom—maybe ask your mate about three sexual fantasy wishes and then grant him at least one. Then surprise him with one of your own fantasies. Add a French tickler to your sex-toy inventory. Do something unexpected: Paint your body red, white, and blue with edible paints. Take a risk. Just do it with energy and spark. This is your time to shine and explode. I guarantee he will, too!

AUGUST

Since there isn't a holiday that falls in August, it's time to create one designed specifically for you and your mate. Maybe it's a variation of your Valentine's Day celebration. Design a holiday that's based on your favorite tricks or sexual needs.

Since the weather can still be hot and sticky, remember: Baths are perfect for every season and every reason. Run the water and pour in the bubbles. One of my favorite cooling items is peppermint soap; it's both invigorating and soothing. You'll feel like one big mint floating in the tub, and the after scent isn't overpowering. Use it to cool off before heating it up with your lover.

Now let's explore the secrets of the kitchen. Sure, we've touched on whipped cream, but everyone uses that! A definite cool tool for August is ice. I know it's nothing new, but it works every time. Set a bucket of ice next to the bed and use the ice to make your lover hot for you. If you enjoy exciting your partner orally, ice will drive him wild. Men love the warm wetness of your mouth. Use the ice to cool him down before you surprise him again with your warm mouth. The contrast of temperature is bound to make him scream. Rub ice all over him, and also try slipping a piece of it in your mouth while you're pleasuring him. It will melt and, within seconds, your mouth will return to ninety-eight degrees of passion.

You can also have you lover rub ice all over your body, paying special attention to your chest and inner thighs. You'll shiver and moan. You'll also crave his warm body all over you. Your mate's fantasies will get the best of him, and he'll try putting ice in places you never dreamed possible. Go with the flow and melt into hot ecstasy while staying cool on the outside.

You can also sit in front of the open fridge door, with your lover blindfolded. Be sure to have lots of sticky, gooey, cool, sensual foods ready to serve: whipped cream, jams and jellies, strawberries dipped in chocolate, frozen grapes, ice cream, oysters if that's a favorite. You'll be hot as the cool air and cool food sends chills up and down your spine.

Fall

SEPTEMBER

Labor Day

I see fall as a time of change, renewal, and comfort. Before you start heating up those hot toddies again, or getting out those bulky sweaters, you have Labor Day, one more warm day for barbecuing, swimming, and relaxing. Hopefully, you and your mate both have the day off, so enjoy the day working on your love life.

We're familiar with all kinds of sex, right? Hangover sex. Make-up sex. Love sex. Morning sex. Funny sex. But on this holiday off from work, enjoy the pleasures of relaxing sex. Don't misunderstand me. It doesn't mean that because you are relaxing that you're not into it! It's slower, more sensual. Spend all day in bed, or by the pool relaxing together, and all that peace of mind will lead you to peace of body with each other. Take it slow, at least in the beginning. Give him a full-body massage as you sit on his lower back completely naked. He'll like the massage, but he'll love the hot body sitting on him. We've too often limited ourselves to back massages. If you haven't gotten, or given, a frontal massage, you're missing out. Situate yourself near your mate's penis without being on top of him. Rub his chest, shoulders and thighs as you work your way all over his body and eventually get on top without taking him inside you yet, even as you get excited and moist in those special places inside your body. If you know your guy well enough and it looks like he's going to climax, then have him massage you first, rubbing your breasts and other areas of your body. Gauge your lover's arousal, and when neither of you can stand it one second more, allow making love to happen as slowly and sensuously as it began. Take time to feel your hands on each other's bodies. Pay close attention to your breathing while also keeping an ear open for his. Breathing is one of the most important indications of approaching orgasm. Stay in sync, and relaxed—take your time; faster isn't always better. Teach your lover by example. When you are on top, avoid the urge to go wild. You'll be amazed by how the sensations feel when you're moving slow and deep. This is a day to relax, without being lazy about your sex life.

OCTOBER

Columbus Day

He was a great explorer. But remember Lewis and Clark? After Columbus discovered America, they got to know the new body of land more intimately. Ask your mate to chart new territory all over your body. You might think that after all these years of having sex, there is nothing new to discover. Honey, you're dead wrong. Our historic world explorers had no idea what they would find after traveling thousands of miles without a specific destination in sight. The key to adventure is what you cannot see. All aboard!

A waterbed makes this adventure even more exciting. If you don't have one, head for the tub. You and your lover will blindfold one another, and explore ecstasy without seeing what's in front of you. Put your blindfolds on *before* you take your clothes off. Make undressing part of the journey. The destination: G land. You might already know where your G-spot is. If you do, congratulations and make sure you do everything you can to guide your lover in the right direction. However, you don't have just one G-spot. There are erogenous zones all over your body—those of you who don't know what I'm talking about, don't worry, you'll soon get the idea.

Halloween

Halloween is the perfect occasion to get kinky with costumes and fantasies. There are hundreds of ways to dress up for a regular Halloween party; our mission here is to dress up exclusively for the sake of sex and fun. Here are a few sexy revisions to some of the most traditional costumes.

NURSE: Bust out of the top, raise the hem, and have a thermometer handy for the hot and feverish.

VAMPIRE: Forget plastic teeth, get the fake caps that stay on for a while. Again, bust out of your cape tied below your breasts. Get pointy high heels and some glossy red lips.

ANGEL: Instead of the long white robe, go for a white piece of lingerie that sparkles. Put a halo on your head, or one over each of your breasts. Don't forget the body glitter and the white satin sheets.

DEVIL: Instead of red pants and a shirt, try a body suit or a red cocktail dress. Don't forget the horns and your three-pronged stake. Glossy lips and red body glitter will help bring out the bad girl in you.

CAT: There is always something sexy about a cat or a kitten, right? Be sure to go for the black body suit or, again, the slinky cocktail dress with a practiced and seductive "meow." No man can resist a pussycat.

NUN: You might have to stick with the long black habit, but it's about what's underneath that counts. And you can make her a naughty nun by stuffing melons in your bra and putting on red lipstick. Underneath that habit, or just behind that slit you added, is a flashy garter and high heels. If you really want to make your lover crazy, wear nothing underneath. You'll win the costume party in his book.

As for trick-or-treating, it's all about tricks for treats in bed. The neighborhood kids can get candy elsewhere: Lock your door and take your fun into the bedroom. The real treat is experiencing the trick, and the best trick is sure to be a treat. Use your costumes as inspiration. Rolf and I have had some of the funniest, and greatest, sex while role-playing. Even though the suggestions above were for you, you can persuade you partner to dress up as the other half. The nurse needs a doctor. The angel and devil have a lot of sexual tension. The nun and priest are bound to mess up once in a while. Cats and dogs bite and scratch each other, and making him bark could be fun.

NOVEMBER

Thanksgiving

The cool months seem to revolve around big meals, and Thanksgiving is probably the biggest. One way to take control of your appetite— and your self-esteem along with it, which is usually quite fragile during the holidays—is to make your own feast. This way you're in charge of the portions and the ingredients. If that's impossible because your mother-in-law insists you come to her house, then volunteer to bring a dish that you will feel comfortable pigging out on.

I know this chapter isn't about weight and diets, but the healthier you feel, the more confident you feel, which means the more daring you can be, which means the better sex you'll have! It's a never-ending cycle that needs attention at every point. So, instead of pigging out too much, and feeling tired and blah after dinner, have just enough to build the energy for later.

By later, I mean another dress-up party in the bedroom, or again, wherever the *Mayflower* may land. The Pilgrims and Native Americans did not share a common language; try communicating with your mate in ways other than normal speech. Use sounds, movements, and hand gestures to tell your mate what you want him to do. It wouldn't hurt, either, if you both dressed your part and played along.

Winter

With the arrival of frigid weather comes warmer clothing. For some plus-size women, it's an excuse to hide in baggy, formless clothing, thinking that all the material will camouflage their bulk. In fact, the opposite occurs and attention is drawn to the extra pounds. Other plus-size women take advantage of winter to layer their clothing: a shawl over a heavy sweater, with a blouse underneath, and then a lightweight sweater—and let's not forget the overcoat for venturing outside. With all those layers, it's a wonder they don't topple over.

Whether it's layering, bulky clothing, or your size, you don't always feel so "hot and sexy" during the winter months. Despite the frost on the windows and the snow-covered lawn, winter doesn't have to be tossed aside as a desexualized season that you simply endure. Maximizing your surroundings also adds to the romantic pleasures of longer nights.

DECEMBER

Christmas

The fire is flickering. Hot toddies are steaming on the coffee table. The kids, and houseguests, are peacefully slumbering. You and your mate sit cozily on the couch, catching your breath. The tree just needs its final touches. Well, you know what? The tree can wait.

Pick up the spare blanket, off the couch, and spread it before the lighted tree. Flick the other lights off, and then make hot-toddy love in front of the tree. You've just created a new tradition, so Merry Christmas!

I understand that Christmas is the season for kindness and goodwill to our fellow man. That doesn't mean your naughty-bad-girl side can't make a special appearance for *your* fellow man. You're an adult now. Santa only cares whether the boys and girls have been good or bad. So be bad, for goodness sakes!

One of my best friends, a mother of three, told me about the kinky Christmas that she and her husband enjoy. On Christmas Eve, after the kids are snug in their beds, and the presents have been placed under the tree, they shed their clothes and become Mr. and Mrs. Claus. They don't bother with the traditional red-and-white outfits, though. Instead, they shop for sexy, Santa-themed lingerie and undergarments. Don't forget the milk and cookies. Now, make it a ho–ho–ho of a Christmas!

JANUARY

New Year's Day

Now that Christmas has passed, New Year's Day is just around the corner, a time for reflection and celebration. It's also a good reason for getting together with close friends, everyone who is important to you. It's how Rolf and I usually spend both New Year's Eve and the day afterward. We make a big party of the night, but it's not about getting drunk and sloppy. To me, New Year's Eve is a time to show appreciation for the good fortune you've enjoyed throughout the past year. It's an opportunity to strengthen the bonds with your mate and your friends. Of course, my favorite time is when Rolf gives me the big midnight kiss just as the clock strikes twelve. Even if you don't have a mate to share the occasion with, socializing with friends is reason enough for celebration. The happy, warm hugs you receive help to make you feel secure.

For years, we attended a friend's New Year's Eve party, in his home. It was a big, splashy production, just as you'd expect in Hollywood. Party guests, all actors and singers, would dance, sing, and perform magic. Those parties were truly memorable nights; everyone had fun and no one got paid.

If you're the ones giving the party, here is a friendly tip to try before the guests arrive. While you're in the bedroom getting dressed, playfully tease one another and continue it—privately— throughout the night. Your guests will be delighted to see their hosts happy and smiling.

When your celebration with friends has ended, make the evening sweeter by arranging an after party for your mate. Your party favors could include hats, candles, masks (preferably feathered), horns, and sparklers. The ultimate party favor is you, as naked as Baby New Year. Let your special guest know that the dress code is very strict: He must also shed his clothing. Rolf and I have done this before. I'll place a feathery mask over his eyes. As I explore his body by touch, I whisper favorite sexual memories we enjoyed together. Modesty prevents me from sharing those special memories, but you get the picture. Invite your man to share *his* favorite memories. Pay close attention to how his body responds, and his breathing. Allow his responses to guide how you touch, kiss, and caress him.

Once you've remembered some past memories, it's time to think about the future. Confide your sexual resolutions for the year ahead. Talk about something you'd like to do for the first time. Offer dates: For instance, "By May, I would like us to make love on a rooftop." Give him a reason to feel excited about the new year. Ask him to share his sexual resolutions. Make an agreement to keep your resolutions. (After all, there's no excuse for breaking *these* resolutions!)

But still, don't forget the present! Make the most of the moment you're sharing together. It's the perfect time to make one of your resolutions a reality. Start the year with a bang, or several bangs, if you so desire!

FEBRUARY

Valentine's Day

This month our little friend the groundhog lets us know if the cold spell will break soon. But there is always Valentine's Day to raise the temperature on February 14. (For those of you who are married, there's a bonus romance holiday. The second Sunday in February is World Marriage Day—a celebration of vowed commitment.)

I keep winter gloom at bay by fantasizing about a tropical paradise getaway. Fresh flowers bloom all around me, and the muggy humidity encourages me to languish in the shower with my honey. Though it exists only in my mind, the beautiful images serve as a springboard to create a tropical paradise in my home.

Surprise the special guy in your life by drawing a bath and filling the bathroom with scented flowers and candles. If you have a small boom box, purchase a tape or a CD of instrumental tropical music, and play the music low. A small fan, also set low, can evoke the sound of a soft breeze. As an extra turn-on for your mate, spray a mist of gardenia oil on your warm body. When your lover comes in to greet you, tell him to undress slowly and slip into the tub with you. Caress his body with flower petals as you rub parts of your warm body against his. Suggest that he rub a flower over your chest, and enjoy the ecstasy of an island lay.

If you want to enhance the romantic setting even further, rent a hotel room for the evening (ideally, find one with a bathtub big enough for two). Send flowers to your mate, along with a note, directing him to meet you at the hotel, where a special surprise awaits him. Since World Marriage Day and Valentine's Day are usually within a week of each other, you can also opt to celebrate the occasions with your tropical treat. Both holidays are opportunities to show your husband how much you love and appreciate him in the bedroom and out of it. Perhaps you could re-create your honeymoon. Book a honeymoon suite at your favorite hotel. Remember what you wore on your wedding night? It probably doesn't fit anymore, so find a look-alike version. What can you recall about it? The music? Drinks? Food? Smells? Utilize anything that helps to evoke your wedding night. You'll be surprised by how much the two of you will laugh as you reminisce about—and relive—that night together. You may even remember sexual fumbles in bed, and how unsynchronized you were. This is the chance to remind each other of how far you've come in your marriage and your sex life. It's quite possible that your wedding night, or honeymoon, was the last time you really went buck wild with your husband. If so, set aside the good-girl role you've been playing and remind him of the "bad girl" who first caught his attention; you haven't lost it, you've merely forgotten to keep it up. Most of us probably take better care of our cars and pets than we do our sex lives. Make World Marriage Day a day of remembering and igniting passions.

But you don't need to spend tons of money on a honeymoon suite. If it's not in your budget, or your realm of reality because you'll need a baby-sitter, a pet sitter, or several days off from work, you can use your home to evoke the first weeks of your marriage. Can you remember what that first night, or week, was like after moving in together as husband and wife? Did you have sex in every room to "break in" the new place? Well, if you didn't, now's the time to do it. If you have a friend or relative to host the kids for the weekend, or even a night, all the better.

When I think of my wedding night, I get warm and tingly all over again! The point is to treasure what's most important: your

marriage. The two of you have come a long way together, emotionally and physically. I've learned that you shouldn't be afraid to *ask*
for this kind of day. Most likely, your mate will have such a great
time, you won't have to ask again. It will become a tradition that
you enjoy annually.

Unfortunately, Sweetheart's Day has become far too commercial and filled with unrealistic expectations. There's so much pressure to make it a perfect day that it can be difficult to have fun and
truly enjoy it for what it's supposed to be, a day when sweethearts
express their mutual affection.

Do you really want a gift he didn't take the time to think about?
How about receiving flowers that he didn't even pick, because they
were ordered by phone? Frankly, my husband is not romantic. I
accept it, and it's okay if he doesn't lavish flowers and candy on me.
Men should feel free to express themselves the way *they* want to.
Valentine's Day isn't a time for laying down the gauntlet and
demanding that your mate prove how much he loves you. When
Rolf does something sweet, like give me the biggest, longest bear
hug in the world, I think it's so much more special than some token
gift that he got all stressed out trying to find. If someone is pressured to do something, then the gesture isn't real. Even worse, men
resent having to act like someone they're not, so don't pressure.

If your husband isn't into buying you sexy lingerie, or reserving
a table at a romantic restaurant, become the initiator and do it yourself. But do it for him, make it come from the heart. If you harbor
resentment, then your gestures are meaningless. I do fun things for
Rolf simply out of love, whether he gets me anything or not.

Chocolate, in particular, is perfect for Valentine's Day. It stimu-
lates nerve impulses and creates a feeling of satisfaction that you're
all familiar with. Believe me, your senses all love chocolate as much
as you do. Its velvet texture, smell, and color all work together to get
you into a warm, fuzzy mood. So, get chocolate candles, chocolate-

dipped strawberries, and some chocolate body paint and let the games begin. If you fear losing control with just one bit, like I do, use chocolate candles or incense as a mood enhancer instead of a butt enhancer. Body paint doesn't have nearly the number of calories as the real stuff. It's easy to spread on and lick off. Feel free to spread it on thick. Chocolate kisses will never taste better!

Candied hearts, teddy bears, and chocolate are the standard things that are supposed to symbolize the sweetness of Valentine's Day. How about spicing it up a bit? This year, make the theme "Sizzling Lust." Move on to red lace, body paint, and sex candy. At specialty stores, you can find intriguing candies that say things like "Touch Me!" instead of the typical "You're sweet." Make up your own sexy sayings and put them on a cookie or a cake; use sugar-cookie batter and red and white frosting to write hot notes to your honey. If you want to avoid sweets, and save the calories for chocolate kisses and body paint, then leave him seductive little notes around the house or office. Think about your sexual inside jokes, fantasies, your body and his, and what you do best together. Possible suggestions: "I want to lick you!" "Make me scream with pleasure!" "Wanna get naked?" "Bold and daring lights my fire!" It's no secret that men enjoy sex, and so do you. This year, instead of flowers, say it with cookies—they can be low-fat and even sugar-free.

Just because you rented a suite, or a hotel room, for World Marriage Day last week doesn't mean you can't go back for seconds. Make Valentine's Day a night to remember by booking a honeymoon suite. Some package deals include fresh strawberries and champagne, satin sheets, huge bubbling tubs, and complimentary fruit (I dare you to discover what other purposes fruit can offer, besides being eaten). If the suite or room doesn't include amenities, bring your personal touch. Earlier in the day, decorate the room so that everything is already in place when you arrive with your lover that night.

Once you've checked in with your tiny overnight bag, unwind with champagne and a luxurious bath or shower. After a soothing and seductive bathing experience, go to dinner somewhere romantic and private. Try touching at all times throughout dinner. It could be with your hands during cocktails, and then with your toes or feet during soup. And don't just play safe with little games of footsie—shock your man by stroking his groin while he's talking to the waiter. Either way, constantly touch each other so that the nerves are ready for sexual sensations later that night. Rolf and I did this once, and as soon as we couldn't stand it another minute, we promptly ended dinner and rushed back to the room, where I slipped into a piece of new lingerie. And then we started all over again.

If you've got kids, then hire a baby-sitter. Even with the responsibilities of being a mother and a wife, and possibly holding down a job, it's important to set time aside for special occasions devoted to romance with your mate. If renting a room isn't possible, be creative with your own space. Maybe it's impossible to find a reliable baby-sitter for Valentine's Day. It doesn't have to undo your special night. Adjust and adapt. The extra effort is worth it.

MOST OF THESE SEXUAL ADVENTURES WILL HAVE YOU BOTH laughing out loud. Laughing doesn't mean it wasn't good sex. It means that your intimacy reached a new level. Sure, the goal is a more exciting and fantastic sex life. But the basis of great sex is communication and intimacy. Many men agree that making love with a woman they truly care about is so much better than a one-night stand. Use these times to rekindle passion, experience lust, and try new things.

Let loose!

Suggested Reading

BOOKS

Burke, Delta, with Alexis Lipsitz. *Delta Style.* New York: St. Martin's Press, 1998.

Cross, Tom Peete. *Lancelot and Guinevere.* New York: Phaeton Press, 1970.

Davis, Elizabeth, and Germaine Greer. *Women's Sexual Passages.* Salt Lake City, Utah: Publishers Press, 2000.

Fein, Ellen, and Sherrie Schneider. *The Rules.* New York: Warner Books, 1997.

Gordon-Wise, Barbara Ann. *The Reclamation of a Queen.* Westport, Conn.: Greenwood Press, 1991.

Jones, Star, and Daniel Paisner. *You Have to Stand for Something, or You'll Fall for Anything.* New York: Bantam Books, 1998.

Korrel, Peter. *An Arthurian Triangle.* Leiden: E. J. Brill, 1984.

Luckett, Moya, and Hillary Radner. *Swinging Single: Representing Sexuality in the 1960s.* Minneapolis, Minn.: University of Minnesota Press, 1999.

Manheim, Camryn. *Wake Up, I'm Fat!* New York: Random House, Inc., 1999.

McCarty, Meladee, and Hanoch McCarty. *Acts of Kindness.* Deerfield Beach, Fl.: Health Communications, Inc., 1994.

Muir, George. *Oprah Winfrey: The Real Story.* New York: Birch Lane Press, 1994.

Neuman, Shirley. *Reimagining Women.* Toronto: University of Toronto Press, Inc., 1993.

Paglia, Camille. *Sexual Personae.* New Haven, Conn.: Yale University Press, 1990.

Pyle, Howard. *The Story of King Arthur and His Knights.* New York: New American Library, 1986.

Stock, Gregory. *The Book of Questions: Love & Sex.* New York: Workman Publishing, 1989.

Tuska, Jon. *The Complete Films of Mae West.* Sacramento, Calif.: The Citadel Press, 1973.

Van Hook, Bailey. *Angels of Art: Women and Art in American Society, 1876–1914.* University Park, Penn.: The Pennsylvania State University Press, 1996.

Weiner, Jennifer. *Good in Bed.* New York: Pocket Books, 2001.

WEBSITES

"A Look at Classical Beauty." http://geocities.com/Paris/LeftBank/6143/bbw.html, 2001.

"All You Ever Wanted to Know about Lilith!" http://www.lilithmag.com/resources/lilithsources.shtml, fall 1976.

"Amazon's Warrior Women or Ancient Myth?" http://tx.essortment.com/amazonswarrior_ryci.htm, 2001.

"Be Attractive the Classic Maya Way." http://www.halfmoon.org/beauty.html, June 2001.

"Circe, Greek Mythology Link." http://has.brown.edu/~maicar/
Circe.html, 2001.

"Dimitri Kare's *Venus on Green*." http://www.fortunecity.com/
victorian/rubens/21/bbw/venusgr.html, 2001.

"Guinevere: Texts, Images, Basic Information." http://www.lib.
rochester.edu/camelot/guinmenu.htm, 2001.

"Mermaids—Undines—Sea Goddesses." http://members.tripod.
com/~ulana7/u3.html, 2001.

"Overview of Lilith." http://ccat.sas.upenn.edu/~humm/
Topics?Lilith/overview.html, 2001.

"Pablo Ruiz Picasso: *Women Running on the Beach*, 1922."
http://www.fortunecity.com/victorian/rubens/21/bbw/
picasso.html, 2001.

"Patrika Darbo." http://www.totofans@Yahoo.com.

"Public Art at UCLA." http://www.usc.edu/isd/archives/la/
pubart/UCLAArt/desnudo1.html, 2001.

"The Culture About Beauty." http://www.beautyworlds.com/
aboutbeauty.html, June 2001.

"Timeless Beauty." http://www.geocities.com/ritterorden/
Liis-Once.htm, 2001.

Acknowledgments

Noreen Reardon for being the best friend anyone could have and teaching me that it's all about attitude. How you see yourself is what really matters.

Heidi Hirsch for her ability to say no to me, and all her fabulous shared artistic abilities; for being another full-figured bitch goddess and true friend.

Patricia Robinson, Anthony Farina, John Moran, and Frances Labyorteaux for giving me fodder and support in writing this book.

Lorraine Zenka for her suggestion that we write this book and for all her shared experiences. She's one hot mama.

All the photographers for making me look fabulous and allowing me to use their photographs: Rosemary Alexander, Rolf Darbo, Michael Papo, John Paschal, Christina Radish, Ann Summa, and Jim Warren.

Nina Wells, Garry Allyn, Corinna Duran, Sean Flannigan, and all my other hair and makeup friends at *Days of Our Lives* for their love, encouragement, and support. They always make me feel as sexy and glamorous as they make me look.

Charles Gannon, the best hair colorist, stylist, and friend. He has always thought of me as one classy, sexy babe.

Days of Our Lives executive producer Ken Corday; Fran Bascom, casting director; and Tom Langan, former executive producer. Without them, this book might never have been written.

Irma Coffey, Lori Boyles, Debra Sanders, Diana Thomas, Maria Le Doux, Lynne Murray, Gloria Gaynor, Paula Sonn, Fary Bjorlin, Paula Cwikly, Janet DiLauro, and Patti Carroll for their friendship, input, and being the hottest, sexiest, and most dynamic group of women I know.

My family for making me who I am; my sister, Peggy, and brother, Danny, for being there in the tough times.

My wonderful fans for their acceptance and support.

Michael Logan of *TV Guide* for proclaiming me one of the "Sexiest People in Television" long before anyone else, and for giving me the title of "Full-Figured Bitch Goddess of Daytime."

Especially my father, Harold "Chubby" Meeks, who called me Queenie until the day he died; my stepdad, Donald Davidson, who told me I could do anything I set my mind to; and my mother, Patti, who deep down did the best she could and who taught me that it was what a woman did, not how she looked, that made her sexy.

Esther Garin, my grandmother, who taught me who I wanted to be and who is blushing, but reading this book with great interest, in the hereafter.

Kevin Spirtas, my costar, for always making me feel sexy and special.

Howie Simon, my publicist, for going above and beyond the call of duty.

Bobbie Edrick, my manager at Artists' Circle Entertainment for always "cutting to the chase" and for being a good friend. My agents at Judy Schoen & Associates, especially Jinny Raymond and Mark Chancer (now at Origins) for making the *Days* deal.

Joel Gotler, my friend and agent, his excellent staff, and that "cute as a bug's ear" Noah Lukeman for all their patience and, especially, their expertise.

Paul Schnee at HarperCollins/Regan Books, a most patient and lovingly efficient editor, and his assistant Ginger Ahn. Likewise, Dana Albarella and Liz Lauricella.

Shari Warren, a beautiful sister in size who can translate the pauses because she's been there, too.

Del Shores for being a good friend and the writer who created some of my best overweight roles because he has been there with us.

And from Lorraine Zenka:

To Patrika Darbo for her willingness to share herself, grow, and let me come along for part of the journey, I'm grateful.

My thanks to Joel Gotler and Noah Lukeman at Artist Management Group who are movers and shakers who have enriched my life; and Justin Manask, who helps me keep my equilibrium with a calming voice.

Our editors, Paul Schnee, for his eye for detail and tender loving care; Dana Albarella, for taking us to the finish line. Their assistants Ginger Ahn and Liz Lauricella.

My warmest appreciation to Robert Waldron, a writer who truly understands, for everything he does to keep me from meltdown. And my parents, Dan and Nellie, for keeping those votive candles lit and in constant meltdown.

My respect for my editorial and research crew: Shari Warren, Jeny Bania, Jane Jost, David Lloyd, Melanie Evangelista, and Judy Barron.

And hugs for Jim Kann for knowing how to love all the woman I am.

About the Authors

PATRIKA DARBO plays the conniving and scheming Nancy Wesley on the daytime drama *Days of Our Lives*. In addition to her work on *Days of Our Lives*, Darbo portrayed Roseanne Barr in the TV movie *Roseanne and Tom: Behind the Scenes*. Her numerous other credits include appearances on the televisions shows *Seinfeld*, *Roseanne*, *Sisters*, and *Grace Under Fire*; and in the feature films *Midnight in the Garden of Good and Evil*; *In The Line of Fire*; *Corrina, Corrina*; and *Babe*, in which she was the voice of the third sheep on the left. A native of Jacksonville, Florida, Darbo lives in Southern California with her husband, Rolf, and their dogs, Rocky and Shooter.

LORRAINE ZENKA is the author of the *New York Times* bestseller *Days of Our Lives: The Complete Family Album*. She has been a West Coast editor of *Soap Opera Update* magazine, and her work has also appeared in *Mademoiselle*, *People*, and *Women's World*.